# FACING THE ABYSS

# FACING THE ABYSS

by

## A. K. CHESTERTON

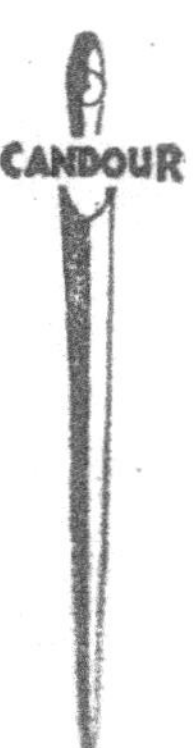


**The A.K. Chesterton Trust**

2014

*__This second edition is dedicated to the British Canadian patriot, John Beattie.__*

*O Lord God, when thou givest to Thy servants to endeavour any great matter, grant us also to know that it is not the beginning, but the continuing of the same unto the end, until it be thoroughly finished, which yieldeth the true glory; through His for the finishing of Thy work laid down His life, our Redeemer, Jesus Christ.*

**Drake's Prayer**

**A.K. Chesterton in April 1969**

© Mirrorpix

# Contents

# FOREWORD TO THE SECOND EDITION, 2014

It is not easy to place *Facing the Abyss* into a single category.

It starts with an analysis of (the fraudulent nature of) party politics and quotes favourably from *The Party Game* by Hilaire Belloc and Cecil Chesterton. They had exposed the sham fights on peripheral issues and consensual silence on the real issues.

In particular, he describes as hypocritical the way in which *The Left* attacks industrial capitalists but regards financial capitalists as being beyond reproach. *The Right*, on the other hand, in the name of the Liberal doctrine of *laissez-faire*, allowed Monopoly Capitalism to flourish at first nationally and then internationally.

He then strays into political philosophy and generously avoids quarrelling with the Brotherhood of Man as a spiritual concept. However, he rightly draws the line at accepting it as a physical and political fact. He grasps the nettle of the innate differences between races and, to a lesser extent, between nations. There is nothing mealy-mouthed about his rejection of the hypothesis of a single undifferentiated humanity. However, neither is there any malice in it.

He is critical of subversion in the universities and even schools and concentrates on the activities of revolutionary students and badly-behaved school children. If he had written the book today, he would have pointed out that some of the revolutionary students of yesteryear were now occupying positions of authority in universities, schools and even Parliament. More worrying is the fact that their nonsensical belief that differences between individuals and between peoples are entirely the product of *nurture*, has now become accepted as incontrovertible fact.

A.K.'s treatment of Hippies and Squares and Mods and Rockers might seem dated but that is largely because the afore-mentioned cults have been superseded by others. It would be more difficult to dismiss his criticism of the hysterical screaming at pop festivals or the uniformly leftist political exploitation of these cults.

His explanation of the Capitalist-Communist Nexus goes beyond the role played by Kuhn, Loeb and Co in the Bolshevik coup, covered in his *New Unhappy*

*Lords*. He explains how the help by Western industrialists to industrialise Russia continued during the 1930s and was, of course, stepped up during the Second World War. His claim of a Communist-Capitalist Nexus was not universally accepted and he recalls a letter published in the *Journal of the Institute of Journalists* dismissing his thesis. It was from a Mr. Sydney Saloman, the publicity officer of the Board of Deputies of British Jews and his letter was published twenty-five years before The Abyss, which was finished in 1973. That would suggest that it was written in about 1948. I shall leave it to others to explore the nature of the complaint and its relevance to the Board.

A.K.'s attack on the 'Partitioning of the World' at Yalta was total and uncompromising and rightly so. Britain's ostensible reason for declaring war in 1939 was the invasion of Poland and yet, at Yalta, Poland and the other countries of Eastern Europe were handed over to a different occupation by the Soviet Union.

His bemoaning the destruction of the British Empire might seem quaint and even irrelevant to some. However, that destruction was not urged to placate the natives but to provide investment opportunities and resources for new heartless exploiters, whose empires would carry no labels.

The 'freedom' enjoyed by the citizens of the newly 'independent' countries of Africa, was of a strangely illusory variety. The benign overlordship of Empire was replaced by the tyrannical and even murderous variety exercised by their fellow Africans.

The official policy of decolonisation was that each newly independent country would be provided with a freshly-designed democratic constitution and that newly enfranchised Africans would elect freshly-moulded Westminster-style politicians who would rule their charges with goodwill, responsibility and innate skill.

A.K. quoted Spengler from *Decline of the West*, with approbation: "It is impossible to impose one culture on another".

One issue that is understated in this book is the one that truly represents 'the abyss' for the nations of Europe. That is immigration and the presence of large numbers of African and Asian immigrants in our midst. A.K. ridiculed the liberal assertion - shared by all of the parties in the Political Class that, "pigmentation revealed no difference of innate psychological dispositions and must therefore be disregarded in determining how the Realm is peopled". However, he seemed to address the issue as though it were merely a symptom of a greater ill.

Of course, A.K. was writing in 1973, when the problem was only twenty-five years old and seemed easily capable of resolution. Now the problem dwarfs all others. Imperialisms can be overthrown; military occupations can be reversed. However, when once the people who created our civilisation are no longer predominant or even in existence, our civilisation will be lost forever.

A.K. would doubtless have seen the international power elites as being responsible for the immigration onslaught and might have seen their defeat as necessary to solving our immigration problems. However, the removal of all of the instruments of the power elite tomorrow would still leave a vast problem for us to solve.

The writing of this Foreword will be one of my last duties as MEP, assuming, that is, that MEPs are responsible for writing forewords! My mandate expires in three days.

**Andrew Brons**

28th June 2014

# PREFACE TO THE SECOND EDITION, 2014

This work was originally entitled *Brutus Over Britain*, but in 1971 when A.K. Chesterton had completed over half of it, he changed his mind at the request of one who he described as "an old friend whose advice he valued", who thought that such a title and theme would cause the message to fall on stony ground because of the reverential credence given to our national Bard's immortal phrase: "This was the noblest Roman of them all". Brutus was left on his undeserved pedestal and A.K. had to begin again.[1]

To our loss, his time came before he could finish the revised book which we now know as *Facing The Abyss*. The final two chapters were completed by his friends using his manuscripts.

The book was serialised in *Candour* from October 1973 before being published in full in December 1976. Although large numbers of the first edition still exist, rusting staples have necessitated a second edition somewhat in advance of schedule. We have corrected some minor spelling mistakes and have taken the liberty of adding a few footnotes when explanations seemed appropriate.

In bringing this second edition to you, we would like to thank Andrew Brons for his foreword, Jez Turner for his enthusiastic help and advice, and Jeff Carson for his proof reading.

**Rob Black & Colin Todd**

The A.K. Chesterton Trust
August 2014


# PUBLISHERS NOTE FROM FIRST EDITION, 1976

A. K. Chesterton died following the completion of Chapter 12 of this book; to complete the book therefore, we have taken the liberty of adding two further chapters taken from his manuscripts — which follow the theme he had in mind — and which, in our view, are a fitting conclusion to this work.

---

[1] Information taken from *Candour*, September 1977.

# FAREWELL TO A.K.

## BY AIDAN MACKEY

Arthur Kenneth Chesterton, M.C., died on Thursday, August 16th, 1973, a month after he was found to be suffering from cancer of the pancreas. He remained in excellent spirits and superb mental form virtually to the end. Only in the last three days were the pain-relieving drugs increased to a level which took him into a sleep and then the final coma in which he died. Until Sunday night he kept hard at work, answering the great flow of letters from friends in many parts of the world, dictating two major articles which appeared in the August/ September issue of *Candour*, and conferring with his closest colleagues about the future of *Candour* and the publication of his new books.

A.K. was born at the turn of the century on the Luipaards Vie gold mine at Krugersdorp on the Witwatersand, South Africa, where his father was Mine Secretary. He went to King Edward's School, Johannesburg, and was later sent to England to Berkhamsted. In 1915, unhappy there and only interested in the war, he persuaded his parents to let him return to South Africa and, immediately upon arrival, he slipped away without their knowledge to enlist in the 5th South African Infantry, exaggerating his age by four years to gain acceptance. Before his 17th birthday he had been in the thick of three battles in German East Africa. Later in the war he was able to transfer to the 7th Battalion Royal Fusiliers, where he served for the rest of the war as a commissioned officer on the Western Front.

In 1918, for conspicuous gallantry whilst leading a series of attacks against enemy machine-gun posts, he was awarded the Military Cross.

For a spell after the war he prospected for diamonds and then joined the Johannesburg *Star*—his first excursion into journalism. In 1922 he was reporting on the Rand rebellion and was very briefly back in uniform, leading a daring and successful attack on the headquarters of the rebels. This marked the end of the insurrection.

In 1924, A.K. came back to England to work on the *Stratford-on -Avon Herald*, and then as editor of the *Shakespeare Review*. When, in the early 1930's, the new Shakespeare Memorial Theatre was opened by the Prince of Wales, his speech was written by A.K.

He edited the *Torquay Times* and other newspapers of the Torquay Times Group, founded the *Paignton News* and wrote several plays, one of which, *Leopard Valley*, was produced in Southport.

In 1933, A.K. married Doris Terry. By then the economic chaos into which Britain was sliding prompted him and many other patriots to join Sir Oswald Mosley in the B.U.F. He became prominent in the movement and edited publications for the Action Press, but quarrelled with Mosley's policies and left the movement in 1938.

When the Second World War started he rejoined the army, volunteered for tropical service and went through all the hardships of the great push up from Kenya across the wilds of Jubaland through the desert of the Ogaden and into the remotest parts of Somalia. He was afterwards sent down the coast to join the Somaliland Camel Corps and intervene in the inter-tribal warfare among the Somalis. It was his experiences with these tribesmen that led to the writing of A.K.'s only humorous book *Juma the Great*[2]. In 1943 his health broke down and he was invalided out of the army with malaria and colitis, returning to journalism.

In 1944 he became deputy editor and chief leader writer of *Truth*, under the fine editorship of Collin Brooks. In April, 1953, he became literary adviser and personal journalist of Lord Beaverbrook and special writer on the Daily Express Group, contributing articles to the *Daily Express*, *Sunday Times* and *Evening Standard*. The relationship with 'The Beaver' was not a smooth one! At the start, A.K. had insisted on honourably working out his notice with *Truth*, and this displeased Beaverbrook. Then *Truth* was bought out and debased by Mr. Ronald Staples, and A.K., determined that its tradition of fearless comment should not be lost, established *Candour*, and his life, for so long dedicated to personal sacrifice for his country, entered its finest and most effective period. Because the money first subscribed was sufficient to cover only printing and basic costs—and that for only a short period—A.K. took no salary, but continued his highly-paid work with Beaverbrook until that too he sacrificed.

---

[2] In fact a second humorous novel does exist and which we hope to publish one day. RB

In the August /September issue of *Candour* was reproduced Sound the Alarm!, the first leading article in *Candour*, which shows how accurately the pattern of attack on the British world had been discerned, and how uncompromising and brilliant was to be the counter-attack. The early months of the paper brought fresh financial support, particularly from R. K. Jeffery, and the small original band of active supporters was reinforced as the little paper grew in circulation and impact.

For twenty embattled years *Candour*, as A. K. Chesterton's platform, has been the foremost weapon in the armoury of not only Britain's defence but that of civilised rule the world over. I do not disparage other journals, here and abroad, if I say that no other editor has approached A.K.'s astonishing perception and almost encyclopaedic knowledge of places, events and people. Time after time I have been present when well-informed public figures from Kenya, Canada, Rhodesia, South Africa, Ireland, the United States, New Zealand, India, Australia and other countries have visited A.K. and have been amazed at his detailed local knowledge, as well as his grasp of major governmental issues in their countries. One such meeting was between A.K. and the Chief Minister of one of the then British lands overseas. The Minister, already taken aback by A.K.'s grasp of the situation which the Minister had just left, was about to tell of a visit and proposals recently made by representatives of the World Bank. A.K. interrupted to say, "No, let me tell you", and as I listened I watched the Minister's face registering ascending degrees of bewilderment and his mouth literally falling open. When A.K. had finished came the response, "But you *couldn't* know that, A.K., nobody knows it yet!", and after he had groped his way into the Croydon night I had to send a taxi after him, bearing his forgotten hat. I repeat that this was no isolated instance.

There is no space now for more. I am certain that our country and the world will find the path back to sanity and some approach to justice. When that happens a great deal will be written about A. K. Chesterton, and the extent of his gifts and his influence will be appreciated. At the moment (I write on the eve of his funeral) those of us who have been privileged to call ourselves his colleagues and friends may be forgiven if, for a while, our grief is less for the loss to our cause than for the passing of a loved friend. We have known not only his public courage and virtues but his personal nobility, his wit and humour, his spiritual and material generosity, and his quite extraordinary patience with those who took up so much of his time with side issues and trivialities.

When I told his old friend and supporter, Henrietta Torrens, that A.K. had died, she quoted to me the lines, from Milton's *Samson Agonistes*, with which the *Morning Post* used to head the Roll of Honour during the First World War:

*Nothing is here for tears, nothing to wail*
*Or knock the breast, no weakness, no contempt,*
*Dispraise, or blame, nothing but well and fair,*
*And what may quiet us in a death so noble.*

Our peoples do not yet know their loss, of what mark of man it is who has gone.

But we know.


**AIDAN MACKEY**

# INTRODUCTION

It is a great honour for me to have been chosen by my late great friend, the author of this book, to write this introduction to it. Although I feel inadequate in the presence of such a beautifully written and thorough a piece of literature, I shall do my best to convey the main points and objectives of *"Facing the Abyss"*.

Although written principally for the benefit of the British people, everything he so eloquently describes is entirely applicable to the United States, perhaps to all Christendom.

You will not get beyond the first few pages when you will realise that what has been happening to Great Britain is precisely the same as that which has been happening to the United States. I can promise you that you will be enlightened and alarmed as patriots and good Americans with the menace which faces us as closely as it does Britain. You will see that we, too, are *Facing the Abyss*.

You will find the truth of treason within our government, the fact that they are deliberately giving their allegiance to a world order which does not officially exist and that this world order is being deliberately created by oppressing and distressing our people by the same group of bankers and monopolists who are wrecking Great Britain. And you will understand the reason for strikes, terrorism and race mixing which are but a preliminary to a dictatorship dedicated to complete enslavement and the loss of our most important treasures by a worldwide conspiracy of financiers and anti-Christians. Napoleon has been quoted as follows: "Financiers have no mother country, no decency, only greed".

**Signed *P. A. del Valle.***

**Lieut. General P. A. del Valle, U.S. Marines (Ret.)**

Chapter 1

# DISEASE BENEATH THE SKIN

So vast is the scope of modern political life, so devious and complex the forces shaping it, that no understanding is possible without the knowledge that seldom does appearance reflect the inner reality. That knowledge, for obvious reasons, is not readily made available. Electorates would be shocked if they became aware that much government is government by false pretences.

Sixty years ago Hilaire Belloc and Cecil Chesterton revealed something of the truth in their book, *The Party Game*, which showed politicians to be engaged in sham fights on issues that were rarely the real issues. These two men had much to do with disclosure of the Marconi contract scandal, which established the involvement of Ministers of the Crown with international capitalist transactions.

Since that time research has been wider and gone much deeper, resulting in the discovery that, in almost all matters of fundamental policy, and not simply in isolated cases, government of the people by the people for the people is a contrived delusion. A more accurate description today is government of the people by the party bosses for international vested interests. The power structure is such that the dominant internal influences are those closely related to the dominant external influences. They are exercised under cover. Those who exercise them are the Lords of misrule who increasingly hold the world in thrall.

Before seeking them out in depth it may help if we examine the general political climate in which our own affairs are conducted and enquire into the sincerity or otherwise of the parties to whom they are entrusted. This does not entail diving below the surface.

Consider, for example, the rise to power — or at any rate to government — of the British Left-Wing. Before and during the First World War its leaders fulminated, not without reason, against the machinations of international finance. Once office was achieved, however, not only did their campaign come to a sudden end, but even the phrase was dropped from their platforms. Why? The reason will in due course become clear. The attacks on "wicked capitalists", of course, continue without abatement at the present day, but care is taken not to differentiate financial capital, which makes debts, from industrial capital which makes goods and which is universally understood to be the target of Left-Wing hostility. In as far as in the upper reaches the two are often married there may be some justification in treating them as one.

While the Bolshevist Revolution was taking place in Russia one of the chief leaders of the Left in Britain, Philip Snowden, was making speeches of such reckless fury that he could blame nobody for thinking that he was himself a violent revolutionary. Within little more than ten years, when he became Chancellor of the Exchequer, he was so beloved by the bankers that they made him a Freeman of the City of London and he ended his career as a peer of the Realm.

Although this transformation was more spectacular (and therefore more ironic) than that of any other colleague, Snowden was not the only "class-warrior" to blaze a path into the exalted world of the Establishment after making a name for himself as its deadly enemy. I know of no Left-Wing politician since the days of Keir Hardie who impoverished himself in the "workers' cause", but hundreds who espoused it and immediately improved the terms of life for themselves as a direct consequence. Such improvement does not of itself indicate personal insincerity, but neither does it betoken any great attachment to the command "Sell all ye hath and give to the poor". The higher the leaders progressed in the hierarchy the wider became the gap in material fortune between them and those (including the poorest in the land) whom they nominally represented. Nobody seemed to mind.

These considerations do not apply only to the Left-Wing leaders of the earlier days. Typical of all too many was the post-war idol whose eloquence rang through the valleys of his native Wales, as — deeply incensed at the suffering of the "underdogs" — he angrily denounced the parasitical capitalists who preyed upon them. Had it been possible to arrange excursions for Welsh miners to come to London for a sight of their champion luxuriously disporting himself amidst the West End flesh-pots they would have recoiled in sheer incredulity. As the man is dead I will not name him. While he was at the height of his popularity I once asked him how he reconciled practice with precept. Scarlet of cheek he could only roar at me: "You see, you cannot help being scurrilous!" It is by no means unknown for Members of Parliament representing working-class constituencies to change into shabbier clothes when going to address meetings in their own area. Such is demagogy.

Other such leaders have simpler tastes, but how many among them lack an eye for the main chance, how many spurn an opportunity to feather their own nests? How many, by stressing the inequalities between rich and poor, have individually widened the gap through their own advancement? It is not "scurrility" which bids me pose such questions, but an earnest desire for the general political scene to be observed other than through rose-tinted spectacles.

The Right-Wing leaders and their Parliamentary followers are infused with hypocrisy of an even deadlier kind. However much or however little their opponents have had to do with the process, there can be no doubt that in purely material terms the standard of living for the large majority of the people of Britain has shown an enormous improvement during the last half century. In so far as this was a Left-Wing aim (and despite any argument that the aim was achieved in spite of its own policies) the Left's apparent claim to success cannot lightly be brushed aside. That in the long term the influence of the Left may prove to have been one of the major factors in plunging the world into the new Dark Ages is another matter and one which we shall consider later. What commensurate triumph can be claimed by the Right? The question presupposes that its main drive is known. If it be known, the secret has been well kept! Should the word "Conservative" mean what one would assume it to mean the Party must seek to conserve, but what it conserves is a mystery when account is taken of what has not in fact been conserved.

As politics — or at any rate political shadow-fighting —became polarised in Britain, the Liberal Party was eliminated as an effective force, its more "radical" elements adhering to the Labour Party and the more "moderate" to the Conservatives. Liberalism in the Nineteenth Century and until the end of the First World War was based on the go-as-you-please policies of the Manchester School. These policies, with certain modifications, were taken over by the Conservative Party, which then became the custodian of the free enterprise system. It has been clear for the last 50 years that, in a country as dependent as Britain on external sources for much of its food and almost all its raw materials, some central planning was essential, but within this broad framework there was vast scope for private enterprise. How well has the Right served as its custodian? The answer is that both the Right and Left have acted as the joint instruments of Monopoly Capitalism within the national context and, as we shall soon see, are now hell-bent on delivering the whole world into the hands of international monopolists. Monopoly, whether public or private, is the destroyer of free enterprise. Thus the Right as the custodian of free enterprise has failed and according to present trends will fail still more disastrously in the future.

Politically the Right is still regarded, against all the facts, as the staunch champion of patriotism and the traditional British values. Not only has it betrayed our national interests and the interests of those who were loyal to us in every part of the world, but it has vied with the Left for the deep dishonour of obliterating the British nation as a separate historical entity empowered to manage its own affairs. It has not only vied, but won. Even this, however, is not necessarily its ultimate betrayal. There is always the possibility of opting out of an international regime when it is recognised as an insupportable and racketeering tyranny set up not for the good of the people but as a means to enable voracious power-addicts to control the world.

The final betrayal of the British nation would be their opting out only to discover that their national identity was no longer Anglo-Saxon and Celtic, but a hugger-mugger of the various strains — African, Asiatic, Italian, French, German, Dutch, Algerian — in fact the lot. To a dangerous extent Britain has already become a province of Cosmopolis.

In 1955 Harold Macmillan, replying to a question of mine, said that he was gravely concerned about the influx of coloured immigrants. Next year he became Prime Minister. From that time until 1964 the immigrant population increased so rapidly that to pass through large areas of the Midlands now suggests driving through Karachi or Bombay, while entire streets and suburbs in London, on both sides of the river, recall the sights and sounds of the Caribbean. Similar patterns have been formed all over the country. As though this were not betrayal enough, the million or so Algerians in France and thousands of Indonesians in Holland will soon have free access to our country, which may also expect the export from Italy of its endemic unemployment problem. A grim prospect.

The politicians of all the Parties, in encouraging or even in tolerating the gift of our island home to swarms of disparate breeds, have been guilty of treason immeasurably more damaging than that of any act for which war-time traitors were hanged. Not for the legislators, however, the prospect of the gallows. Let them but continue to subserve the dominant influences at work undermining our nationhood and if they do not secure a seat in the House of Lords, as well they may, there is always the chance of a knighthood to console them.

In the consideration of such matters it is only fair to the Left to say that, since the days of Robert Blatchford, it has never pretended to be other than anti-patriotic. Its wan, thin-blooded, priggish little leader in the 'thirties, Clement Attlee, was proud to boast that he and his colleagues were deliberately giving their allegiance to a world order (which did not happen to exist) and not to their own country. His present-day successor, the egregious Harold Wilson, has loftily declared the whole world to be his kin — a ludicrous concept, but not ludicrous enough, it would appear, to evoke the derisive laughter of his followers.

The Right can make no such general claim to excuse their manifold treasons. As they claim to be patriots most of them trade under a fraudulent label and do so unblushingly because they know that the traditional Conservative image handed down from a nobler past is firmly implanted in the minds of their followers. As labour voters look upon the Labour Party as their bulwark of defence against the "wicked capitalists", so do the old dears (of whatever age) look upon the Conservative Party as their bulwark against the depredations of the "wicked socialists". Both images are false.

What goes on in the minds of Right-Wing M.P.'s intelligent enough to be aware of what their leaders are doing? In the middle 'fifties Captain Henry Kerby, Conservative M.P. for Arundel, asked me to visit him at the House of Commons. His object was to tell me that he and very many of his colleagues greatly admired the work I was doing in defence of British interests at home and overseas. I expressed my gratification, adding that it would be even more encouraging were the Members to defend these causes from the floor of the House. "Never fear, A.K. never fear, it will come, it will come" he assured me. The years went by but nothing came. Then it occurred to me to ask why, if the others were afraid to speak out, Kerby did not himself defy the Devil.

Here, as far as I can remember, was his answer: "Look, all the chaps on our side of the House, if they do not possess private means, have this, that, or the other City directorship, or are political advisers to this or that big corporation. Some of the biggest corporations have quite a bevy of political advisers, and not all from our Benches! For my own part I have no City directorship or emoluments from any outside source. If I were to stand up in the House and hammer home the truths you publish, Central Office would not lose a day before getting to work in my constituency. Somebody else would be put forward as the official candidate at the next election and I would be ditched".

There was nothing more that I could usefully say, so I kept my thoughts to myself. Henry Kerby and I remained friends for the remainder of his life and in many ironic little notes to me he expressed his views on the Parliamentary scene. Some were very brief. "Did you see what Tufton B. said in the House yesterday? A knighthood for him!" "So the first Suez rebel has begged the second batch of Suez rebels to return to the fold. Mark my words, it will be 'Arise Sir Harry' ". His prognostications were never wide of the mark. Only once, however, did Kerby take the initiative in Parliament. He tabled a Bill for the reform of the monetary system, but even if he had not been in declining health I doubt whether he would have pressed it home with vigour. Henry Kerby was a charming man and completely sincere in his outlook. The thought sometimes came into my mind that charm and political sincerity need not debar their possessor from a post in Intelligence.

Kerby's ironical contemplation of his colleagues in Parliament shows something of the reality of life in the Palace of Westminster, as it does the unreality of many popular conceptions of what takes place there. While it cannot be said that the politician is a greatly esteemed figure in modern Britain few people realise how great is the difference between Parliamentary values and the values upheld in private life. As a private person, for instance, it is most improbable that Julian Amery would take a very strong line against some business issue, and then — without there being any objective change — turn round to defend it. A Suez rebel, he denounced the Government's policy in no uncertain terms: immediately afterwards, promoted to a Ministerial post in the War Office, he arose in Parliament to speak in its defence. The course of action he took was not due to a change of mind. His new duties required it of him. This seemed as natural to him as it did to everybody else in the House. In due course when Sir Julian is bidden to arise, beyond doubt he will do so with the consciousness of having rendered valuable political services to the country. Distinction between country and party is not a line which the casuists of Westminster trouble to draw.

There is also an atmosphere in Parliament which has a vitiating effect on all but the strongest characters. As pressures through the year have multiplied, so has the atmosphere been intensified. Today moral courage, the readiness to take a determined stand in the face of general displeasure, the resolve at all costs to be a man in his own right and not simply a cog in a Party Machine — these attitudes are rarely encountered and even more rarely for long maintained.

It may be that the difference between public and private life in some respects is quantitative rather than qualitative. Both appear to suffer from the same disease — a disease which assumes its most virulent form in Parliament. Despite its name, it does not set free but enslaves the human will, confining its activity within the limits of what is permitted, which means usually all things which paralyse, stultify or degrade but nothing that would stand athwart the New Barbarism's stampede into chaos.

The name of the disease is liberalism, a corrosive poison.

Chapter 2

# THE LIBERAL DISEASE

Liberalism, spelt with a small "l", is partly an induced frame of mind and partly a product of social fatigue which leads its victims to feed on catchwords and slogans in preference to thought. The next step is the basing of policies upon the foundation of the Dreamland conjured up by the slogans, which then become false symbols creating a world of total unreality. The denizens of this unreal world are rendered easy prey for the Lords of Misrule.

First among the current slogans which undermine social stability is the term "The Brotherhood of Man". This is a spiritual concept with which there is no reason to quarrel. The mischief only arises when it is accepted as a physical and, at the next remove, as a political fact. In such contexts it is nonsense. At best it presupposes an affinity between all men, irrespective of whether or not it exists. Neighbours sharing the same way of life may have close enough affinity to become friends, or just enough to be friendly acquaintances. On the other hand they may be, like most city-dwellers, neutral for lack of any such consciousness, or else antipathetic to the point of loathing. Kinship in a more general and less personal sense nevertheless transcends these considerations where there is a shared identity, national, tribal or even social. This identity it is the concern of liberalism to smash.

National identity assumes the same broad historical experience, the sense of "belonging", more often than not the same language and more or less the manifestation of the same national characteristics. "More or less", because in such matters there is no absolute. Not all Italians are volatile, but there is such a thing as Italian excitability. Not all Englishmen are calm, but Anglo-Saxon phlegm nevertheless exists. That national identity does not exclude affinity between nations sharing the same cultural values scarcely requires to be stressed: were it otherwise the appreciation of Shakespeare would be confined to English-speaking people and only German ears would be attuned to Beethoven. The shared delights of peoples of the same culture group nevertheless do not detract from the reality of distinctive national identities.

The liberal either ignores this truth or makes light of it. Because men the world over have the same biological functions they hold that there is no essential difference between them, which is about as reasonable as saying that because the black mamba and the spitting cobra are both snakes they cannot be differentiated.

These liberals, however learned in other spheres, are superficialists when they seek to turn the spiritual concept of the brotherhood of man into a physical concept and base upon it a political principle. Their favourite argument is that to assess a man by the colour of his skin is an iniquity, as indeed it would be if there were no other differences and if what lay beneath the skin—the mental qualities and what may perhaps be called the psyche—were qualitatively the same in mankind as a whole. But this is not true. Pigmentation is no more than an outward manifestation of profounder differences between the races. That there can be close co-operation between races is well established, that the basic emotions of hope and fear are a common factor is in general true, and that personal loyalty can transcend racial boundaries has often been proved.

But the fundamental differences remain. No people are more aware of them than the Chinese. To the Chinese, although they may no longer proclaim it, all aliens are "foreign devils". There is abundant evidence that Chinese women regard physical contact with European men with revulsion.

The recent attempts of the Australasian Governments to bring the Pacific Islanders into some kind of federal organisation met with horrified resistance. Cook Islanders were not prepared to merge with Samoans, the inhabitants of Samoa were disdainful of being identified with those of Niue and the peoples of New Guinea would not even tolerate the mixing of tribes inhabiting the same homeland.

Awareness of identity is a human characteristic. It does not constitute an absolute, in that it changes with the changing of national allegiance, although even then it can long survive—the Irish tend to retain their Irishness in the USA and many Americans are proud of their English or Scottish ancestry.

Identity finds expression in action and it is here that it becomes most marked. Thus the main European nations, each in its own distinctive way, produce brave fighting-men who do not shrink from dying on the battlefield as a normal wartime hazard. But the bravery does not take the form of deliberate acts of suicide: for that kind of fanatical courage one has to refer to the Japanese airmen who flew their aeroplanes upon enemy warships with the certainty of blowing themselves up on impact. The liberals would argue that such fanaticism is the result of indoctrination. It is nothing of the kind. Few indeed are the Europeans who could be "conditioned" to undertake enterprises which held no chance whatever of personal survival. The factor here is the relative value placed on the individual life in relation to the life of the community. Conditioning can go a long way in the Western world, but it cannot go all the way in destroying the will to live.

In spite of these considerations, the liberals in Britain (who have made an almost complete conquest of the three established political parties) have so influenced policy that it proceeds on the "Brotherhood of Man" basis, which is that pigmentation reveals no difference of innate psychological dispositions and must therefore be disregarded in determining how the Realm is to be peopled.

We shall have more to say on this vitally important subject in a later chapter, but before leaving it here, one example of its dangers and a general reflection may not be out of place. In 1971 an immigrant appeared before a British magistrate charged with sexual assaults on two small English girls aged 12 and 11 respectively. The magistrate found him guilty, but imposed a suspended sentence, explaining that he did so because what the man had done was not a criminal offence in his country of origin. Similar magisterial remarks in different parts of the country strongly suggest that there has been a Home Office directive covering such matters. If so, the action is infamous, as it totally disregards the rights of Britons to the protection of their government.

The general reflection is this. Our forefathers through the centuries have exerted themselves, with complete success, to keep the British Isles inviolate, and with almost complete success to merge into a British nation, with its distinctive values and traditions, the Anglo-Saxon and Celtic peoples who are its true inhabitants. The men and women of my generation fought two most bloody wars in the belief that they were preserving the historical British entity. What has happened that the labours of the centuries, culminating in the prodigious sacrifices of our own time, should have been so derided by the result?

There are many other aspects of the liberal influences at work destroying our national sovereignty and heritage. One is the assumption that, as there should be no racial barriers within the United Kingdom or anywhere else, so should there be no national frontiers. Their ideal is One World, governed by a central authority with sole power of military and police, of taxation, of law-giving and of imposing upon mankind the same general standards, the same pattern of life.

The people who entertain this remarkable idea, the charming old ladies (of both sexes) who form United Nations Associations and similar bodies, have clearly succumbed to the euphoria created by the magic spell of phrases such as the "Brotherhood of Man". Their hearts do them more credit than their heads, for in simple truth they can never at any time have thought out the implications of what they support. The phrase gives the comfortable glow of depicting the human race, with all its disparity, settling down in harmony to live the good life as one people, single and indivisible. Their benign faces light up as they explain that there will be no more wars, no more contending for power — nothing to prevent the immediate ushering-in of the millennium.

By reason of their naive enthusiasm, these people are being ruthlessly exploited by the power-addicts who have already, through money-manipulation and other means, secured a merciless grip on human affairs, and who will not be content until they achieve the complete political, economic and strategical masterdom of the world. That they will meet with total success is not assured, but one thing is certain —the nearer they approach to their goal the more hideous will become their oppression. One World could only be run as an all-embracing Communist tyranny. Secret police would be everywhere, to pounce at the smallest hint of opposition. That the worthy upholders of "good causes" should be unable to perceive where their dreams must lead is yet another example of the truth that the ideal is the enemy of the real. Were they even to catch a glimpse of reality they would be able to discern, as stages towards World Government, the design behind the setting up of such bodies as the European Economic Community.

The most widely diffused influence of liberalism is found at present in our domestic affairs. In recent years it has been responsible for creating ever-increasing irresponsibility, particularly among the youth of the nation. As its tenets are rarely defined, it has to be judged for the most part by its effects on society. These indicate a breakdown of discipline, not so much as a side-effect as a conscious objective. Any kind of restraint is scorned. Hoodlums are often supported when they rampage through the streets, to turn sporting events into a riot and to try to the uttermost the patience of the police, whose efforts to control unruly mobs lead to instant complaints of "brutality" and who are given the amiable title of "pigs". Outbreaks of this kind tend to be regarded as fortuitous, but the similarity of the pattern they have begun to assume throughout the Western world is clear evidence that they are being master-minded.

It should not be thought, however, that the lack of social discipline and sense of responsibility is confined to youth. Industrial strikes, which have become more or less endemic in the present century, at one time had every justification as the only means whereby labour could resist its ruthless exploitation by the "captains of industry". Those times, however, are long past. The balance has swung so far the other way that today the withholding of labour has power to inflict damage on the national economy which could be irreparable. Fully aware of this power, the wielders of it tend all too often to become the new exploiters, making preposterous wage demands which are often pressed home by use of the strike weapon, even though the result be to make war, not only upon a particular management group but upon the entire nation, completely without regard to the miseries inflicted upon fellow-workers in other occupations. In this tough world no community can survive indefinitely faction fights conducted without regard to the public good.

Leaving out of account industrial relations, which constitute a separate problem, and which have been mentioned here only to indicate the perils of irresponsibility, we return to the question asked about why the labours of the centuries to create, and the fearful blood-letting of two world wars to preserve, the national and racial identity of the British peoples should have met with such catastrophic and derisive results in the second half of the present century.

The only answer that makes sense is — betrayal.

# Chapter 3

# LANGUAGE OF BETRAYAL

The cry "We have been betrayed," so familiar to the French, has seldom been heard on British lips, although not for lack of cause. During the last hundred and fifty years or more we have been governed by deceptions so unsubtle that they would have been dashed to pieces on the rock of French realism. We are among the easiest people in the world to beguile. Politics has been defined as the art of the possible, but in Britain it should be redefined as the art of the possible in extending human credulity or nullifying human incredulity, which gives it a boundless range.

Instances abound. Winston Churchill's statement that he would act as Roosevelt's "loyal lieutenant" received wide publicity, but when it became known that he had thus pledged himself only a few weeks after accusing Roosevelt of being intent upon the destruction of the British world system, nobody in public life discerned any incongruity in these attitudes. In the same way Churchill gave his fellow-countrymen much comfort and reassurance when he said that he had not become His Majesty's First Minister to preside over the liquidation of the British Empire. The fact that when he finally laid down the seals of office the Empire had virtually ceased to exist in no way detracted from the stupendous legend which had grown around him.

The final example, for present purposes, was the formula which enabled overseas governments, in repudiating allegiance to the Crown, to recognise the Monarch as "Head of the Commonwealth." This gave most Britons complete satisfaction, which may or may not have been shared by the politicians. The only statesman who, recognising that the words were devoid of meaning, publicly described them as "nonsense" was an Afrikaner loyalist, General Smuts. It will be useful to bear these instances in mind when we come to deal with the policies of Harold Macmillan, Harold Wilson and Edward Heath.

Although easy to deceive the British, their gullibility to some extent stems from what at one time was regarded as the main national characteristic, symbolized by John Bull and the bulldog. What the bulldog grips it will not lightly relinquish. Writing of our people soon after the First World War, the distinguished American author William Bolitho said that what they had, they held. This view is long out-dated — except in one sphere. Despite floating voters, despite electoral swings this way or that, the bulk of the electorate will hold on like grim death to party allegiances as long as they remain polarised. Most countries have several parties in their legislative assemblies. In Britain, as the Liberals can attest, there is only room for two at the top. Members of non-Establishment groups with a livelier sense of present realities and perils may put up candidates and, in the course of canvassing, convince voters that the dangers to their country are very real and menacing, yet when the ballot-box is reached those voters can rarely bring themselves to act in the light of that conviction: party loyalty is too strong within them, not because of party policy, but because the party label has become for them a personal possession to be prized. What they have they hold! This tenacity, so admirable in other fields of human endeavour, is one of the chief factors betraying Britain to its doom.

The shifting stance of the parties themselves is another of the curious phenomena of our times. Trotting out the old unhallowed catch-phrases, "class-enemies," "those dreadful socialists" or whatever it may be, the parties nevertheless constantly change their ground. What is more, the direction itself tends to be constant — leftwards.

Why this should be is difficult to analyse. The superficial explanation is that the movement conforms to public opinion, but, while the public may take its cue from the B.B.C. and the Press, it has precious little to do with the formulation of opinions, which often enough go contrary to their own — until at last usage wears them down. The originators of "fashions of thought" are not to be found in Fleet Street or the B.B.C. whose denizens are mere line-pluggers. Those who provide the line are those who have a vested interest in its acceptance.

That the technique succeeds cannot be questioned. There are Conservatives known to me who thirty years ago would have proclaimed themselves ardent Imperialists but who today would run a mile from any such avowal. "Imperialism" and "Colonialism" (a meaningless fabrication) are now swear-words as venomous as "Fascism". But who made the decree that words acceptable to one generation should be hateful in the ears of the next?

Americans in particular are vehement in their denunciation of both "Imperialism" and "Colonialism", which must be accounted strange. If the United States of America are not based upon the early colonial settlements, whence is one to look for their origin? Should they regard their beginnings with shame, why do they not decry the voyage of the *Mayflower* and hold their Founding Fathers in disdain? There is much hypocrisy in this matter, which unfortunately has to some extent rubbed off on native Britons. Both people are happy enough to talk, say, about the "American colony in London" or of the "British colony in Rome." The word itself is a perfectly good one.

When I was a very young soldier in the First World War it was an honour to serve with the "Colonial Forces", as Australian, Canadian, New Zealand, South African and Rhodesian troops were called. They provided some of the very finest storm-divisions in the British army. It was no less an honour to serve with the "Imperial Forces", which is how the colonial soldiers referred to units raised in the United Kingdom. We have indeed been sadly lacking in vigilance that political jackals, for their own ends, have been enabled to bring once honourable names down to the gutter-level of scorn and abuse.

The attacks on "Imperialism" are no less hypocritical. Ever since the dawn of history, and probably since the advent of man, there have been mass movements of people across the surface of the earth. Europe itself has known countless waves of migration, as have other continents. The main races of the Indian sub-continent are not native there. The Maoris are not native to New Zealand but comparatively recent newcomers. The Bantu are not native to South Africa. Msilikatzi, who broke away from the Zulu power in the first half of the last century and blazed a blood-sodden path over a thousand miles of territory to establish his warriors as the Matabele nation is honoured by the B.B.C., and the Westminster politicians, who yap at Rhodesia, take good care never to mention the unbridled Matabele savagery which prevailed there before the coming of the European settlers.

It would seem that to warrant the opprobrious title of "Imperialist" a nation must send its settlers overseas. As long as its sway is extended to contiguous lands all is accounted well and may even be considered admirable. Americans are proud of their frontier days and express no regret that in pushing it ever westward they systematically deprived the Red Indians of their territories. Being in their own eyes a very special people; they find nothing culpable in having seized further vast areas from Mexico and Spain. Understanding, as I do, the drive to expand, there is no thought in my mind of condemning these conquerors. What does horrify me is the sheer humbug of their descendants in sitting in judgment upon sea-faring inhabitants of the British Isles for carrying their flag, their language and their civilisation to the ends of the earth and who in doing so founded the North American nations.

That the Russians should compete with the Americans in the virulence of their attack on "Imperialism" is even more nauseating. If it be a sin for the British to settle in New Zealand or Rhodesia or anywhere else, what is to be said of the pre-revolutionary rulers who stretched far beyond the Urals to bring the huge land-mass of Central Asia within the Tsarist domain? Perhaps the excuse of contiguity also serves to protect Russia from the "Imperialist" smear, but that again is a mere abuse of words. As no well-defined and established nations were included in the take-over, there will be little disposition to make retrospective protests over annexations of that kind. But the same thing cannot be said of the seizures carried out by the successor Red regime. To describe them as "Imperialist" would be to insult the imperial theme. No infamy in human annals can have exceeded the wickedness of occupying the Baltic States and transporting the entire bulk of their effective citizens thousands of miles to an unknown fate in the wastelands of Siberia. That today the slogan mongers of the Soviet Union should shout abuse at so-called "Imperialists" while holding in their iron grip nations immeasurably superior to them in culture and civilised behaviour — Poland, Czechoslovakia, Hungary, Eastern Germany, Bulgaria and the rest — is more obscene than any language has words to describe.

We shall discover in due course how close has been the co-operation between the Americans and Russians in dispossessing the British and other European nations of their overseas territories and spheres of interest, but it should already be apparent that their joint use of anti-Imperialist jargon has long been at work influencing the thought-processes of the British people, creating in them a wildly irrational "guilt-complex" from which they do not themselves suffer on account (at any rate in the Soviet case) of outrages against other States which should induce feelings of blackest guilt.

As the British Labour Party — the self-acknowledged party of anti-patriots — has played the most dynamic part in shaping the British habits of thought (or more accurately of feeling) since 1917 or thereabouts, it must be held responsible for the climate of opinion which has caused Britain's post-war impotence. However much most of its members may detest the Communist challenge, they have nevertheless allowed themselves to become the mouthpieces of Communist propaganda directed against their own country. Conservatives for their part have come increasingly to rely on a bogus "special relationship" with the United States whence they have been contaminated by much the same influences. Hence the leftward movement of British policy. Hence the shedding of our overseas responsibilities. Hence the present flight from nationhood itself. When the Central African Federation was about to break up, Mr. Duncan Sandys, then in charge of the Commonwealth Office, told Sir Roy Welensky that the British had lost the will to govern. Acquiescence in Heath's stampede into Europe would suggest that the Conservatives have lost the will to govern even their own country.

That gigantic financial and other pressures have been brought to bear to ensure British surrenders at home and overseas cannot be denied. The fact remains that the pressures would have failed had the British spirit not been sapped — and sapped by mere words. Victorious in war, our nation is now being overthrown, not by guns, but by the language of betrayal.

Chapter 4

# SUBVERSION IN THE UNIVERSITIES

One of the recent methods of befouling the concept of nationhood in Great Britain, as in the other Western countries, has been the political exploitation of youth. This is a pernicious trend and in at least one instance has led to catastrophe. I refer to Northern Ireland. While this unhappy part of the United Kingdom is no stranger to violent upheaval caused by religious antagonism, it was not religion which sparked off the latest frenzied warfare, but the activities of a totally unprepossessing young Continental who, after achieving banner headlines in the world's press, disappeared into the obscurity where he belongs. His name is Cohn-Bendit[3] and he first made his mark in what from the first should have been dismissed as a freakish escapade.

Associated with the Sorbonne in Paris is another college at Nanterre. It occurred to the students at the latter establishment that it had a duty to make accommodation available for young men and women who might wish to sleep together. When the authorities rejected the demand Master Cohn-Bendit started a riot. The rioting spread rapidly to the Sorbonne, whose students forcibly occupied the University premises. By this time the original cause had been pushed into the background and was lost from view when pretty well the entire labour force of France downed tools to join in the fun. For several days there was anarchy.

The originator of these frolics then formed a ginger-group to act on an international scale. There were fun and games in Bonn. Then operations were switched to London, where a rabble was incited to attack the United States Embassy, which resulted in what became known as the Battle of Grosvenor Square, where the police more than held their own at a cost of only a few helmets and one or two minor injuries. The same kind of situation was created in Belfast, but here the repercussions were lethal.

Because of the history of strife in Northern Ireland, it was no difficult task to raise hell, but emphasis must be laid on the fact that the motivation in the first place was not religious hatred but political agitation inspired by the Nanterre-

---

[3] Daniel Cohn-Bendit has been a federalist (and controversial) Member of the European Parliament since 1994.

Sorbonne outburst and developed by the left-wing Civil Rights Movement. That the I.R.A. exploited the situation is of course true, but the idea that this terrorist organization is motivated entirely by Irish patriotism is fallacious — a large segment of its core is revolutionary in the left-wing sense of the word.

Elsewhere, with no basic antagonism to feed on, rioting started by the Cohn-Bendit "warriors" was sporadic and —except in the United States — did not call for military intervention. Nevertheless another element had made itself felt in Western politics. In an effort to discover what philosophy animated its originators (or perhaps to broadcast their views!) the B.B.C. invited Cohn-Bendit and about a dozen choice and master spirits among his entourage to take part in a television interview, which must have amazed all who saw it. As they sat in horseshoe formation, the interviewer gave each an opportunity to speak. Some were tongue-tied, others delivered themselves of vapid mush and from not one emerged the ghost of an idea. Their leader proved as inane as his followers. Perhaps his horizon extends no further than his Nanterre grievance! The programme was a fiasco.

It was this weird bunch which introduced to the British people what is now universally known as the New Left. Fragments of it had long been familiar, but today they are seen as lambkins bleating in one and the same pen — Trotskyists, Syndicalists, Maoists, Che Guevarists, Castroists, Anarchists, Young Liberals — the entire greasy-haired array of modern class-warriors. If anybody has ever thought of analysing what shades of difference distinguished them, I for one am not interested in discovering the result! Somewhat later, Cohn-Bendit's elder brother, who seems to have been the "intellectual" of the outfit, produced a rather incoherent treatise, a strange mixture of Marxist generalities and undigested Sartre Existentialism, which was supposed to serve as doctrine but which seems to have fallen into the bottomless void. Apart from that, the only definition I have heard was a statement by a South African adherent, who said: "Our policy may be summed up in two words — 'Perpetual Revolution' ". There may be people to whom that statement makes good sense, but I am not among them. To my mind it is the policy statement of a maniac.

Yet the New Left exists. The explanation may be that in recent times the Soviet Union has sought a more respectable "image" and accordingly discourages Communist Parties in the West from overt association with civic tumult and any activity other than infiltration and industrial unrest. This does not mean that Moscow looks with disfavour on others willing to act in its stead. These others, seething with a revolutionary fervour which lacks all rationale, for their part had come to look upon the local Communist Party as part of each Western Establishment and in disdain branched off on their own, each taking the "ism" which he most fancied.

The movement in its own right is not, and can scarcely hope to be, of any high political importance, but one truth it has discovered, or perhaps more accurately re-discovered, is the availability of university undergraduates for purposes of revolutionary demonstrations. It may justly take the credit for what other generations would have regarded as an impertinent imbecility — Student Power. Undergraduates are necessarily a transient population and when they go out to face the world many of those classed "militants" leave behind them such childish day-dreams. The point is that others take their place, so that at any one time the universities always have their quota of adolescents passing through a phase when they can be utilised for subversion.

Following the Sorbonne uprising, the standard of revolt was unfurled on almost every campus in the western world. Some of it may have been centrally organised, some of it imitative. "Grievances" varied from one country to another, but throughout there would appear to have been a central tenet. This was that the taxpayers should meet the cost of their university training, should pay them salaries for graciously allowing themselves to be educated and consent to their virtually taking control of the universities, deciding what they should be taught and who should teach them. This was the underlying motif, although the immediate cause of their demonstrations would usually be local grievances, varying from campus to campus. The normal method was the "protest by posterior." Taking possession of buildings, the students sit down on the floor and refuse to budge. Sympathetic or sycophantic lecturers, and even professors, sometimes plonk down academic rumps in their midst. This kind of demonstration was first made popular by the Campaign for Nuclear Disarmament marchers whose aim was to destroy Britain's means of protecting herself in a world of ever increasing violence and hostility and whose favourite tactic was to favour Whitehall with the imprint of their bottoms. Such behaviour would seem to belong to the all-prevailing decadence, as it does not accord with the dignity of man, which requires him to express his beliefs standing erect on his own two feet.

Student revolutionary groups are not a new phenomenon, but never before have they formed the nucleus of a movement stretching throughout the West, from

Macgill in Canada to Sydney, from Chicago to Cape Town, from London to Auckland. What is more, the Western pattern everywhere is the same — anti-nationalist, anti-patriotic, racial-integrationist and all using the identical political jargon. The Fabian Society, which many years ago proclaimed its policy of infiltrating such institutions, has done its work well. That the result is approved in the realm of High Finance may be deduced from the encouragement given by Mr. Harry Oppenheimer, multi-millionaire associate of the Rothschilds. As Chancellor of the University of Cape Town he told a large assembly of undergraduates in Natal how delighted he was that students should have become so active in demonstrating and making known their views. What knowledge of life these young men and women, with nothing but their school-days to guide them, can bring to the shaping of contemporary thought and action is perhaps a secret locked in the Oppenheimer breast. One suspects, that he would be able to resist the temptation to hand into their keeping the management of his Anglo-American and de Beers companies, his chain of newspapers or any other of his uncountable business interests throughout the world.

Particularly shocking to Britons who retain any sense of national pride is the knowledge that Yahoo behaviour, so far from being confined to the new "red-brick" universities, has reached its lowest depths in those once proud and world-famous seats of learning — Oxford and Cambridge. The long, greasy locks, the disgusting face-fringes, the cheap and nasty jeans — all the distinguishing marks of Hippydom — are as frequently encountered here as they are in any other university town, but it is not simply a matter of appearance. Because some frenetical young hoodlums at Cambridge did not like the orderly regime in Greece, they had no compunction in storming a hotel in the neighbourhood in an attempt to wreck a dinner-party being given in honour of a Greek diplomat. Since that time the authorities have narrowed the bounds wherein University discipline holds sway, thereby shrugging off responsibility for any such event in the future.

Oxford has acquired an even less savoury reputation. Instead of being accorded every courtesy, as in the past, guest-speakers whose views do not coincide with those of unwhipped whelps, who understand nothing about the realities of the world, run every risk of being mobbed and seriously injured. Not long ago, Callaghan, the Chancellor of the Exchequer, was invited to address the Oxford Union. Although a Socialist, he did not stand far enough to the Left to please the rabble organised to scream him down. Within a few minutes of his rising to speak, the President of the Union abandoned the meeting, because — as he told reporters — the proceedings had been reduced to "total chaos." Some days later it was revealed that less than 7% of those present had taken any part in the uproar, which fact brought to many people a surprising comfort. Neighbours of mine said, almost in triumph: "So you see hooliganism at Oxford is not as extensive as you think!" That attitude astonished me. I replied: "If the entire audience had consisted of hooligans, what took place would have been natural. To my mind it is altogether horrifying that over ninety-three per cent had come along to listen to a speech and supinely allowed a small thug minority to prevent its being delivered. Why did they not bestir themselves to kick the wreckers out into the night? Were they afraid?"

The answer is probably that it was not physical fear which inhibited the overwhelming majority of those present from taking action, but something almost as deplorable — the disinclination to be involved. It is from this silent majority in the world at large that the greatest threat to national survival is to be feared. If the great mass of people are prepared to remain inactive whenever small groups of thugs set out to ruin their pleasure, their tolerance is not the friend of freedom but its enemy. The disquieting factor is that, accepting as it does the evil that is physically manifest, such tolerance concedes victory at the start to evils not thus manifested. This no doubt explains why the modern world suffers itself to be dominated by evil influences.

The universities, with submission, are not doing their duty if they make no attempt to inculcate those they send out into the world with a sense of responsibility to the nation which has bred and educated them — a sense of responsibility strong enough to overcome any disinclination for personal involvement. They should be the citadels of patriotism, which is the spiritual force which binds a nation together. In recent years they have allowed bumptious young prigs to turn them into nurseries of anti-patriotism, and if this has been done in the face of official displeasure the public is not aware of the fact. Indeed the general impression whether fair or unfair, is that many authorities, themselves steeped in liberal rot, impart their own false values to their students. Should this not be the true explanation, then they can scarcely claim success in their discouragement of the anti-patriotic cause.

For instance, while British soldiers were being killed or wounded in the thankless task of trying to keep order in Northern Ireland, not a murmur of indignation was heard issuing from Oxford, Cambridge or any other British university. But when the Parachute Regiment, confronting a dangerous situation in Londonderry, was forced to fire upon gunmen and thirteen people were killed, screams of rage rang through innumerable campuses, and two hundred and fifty frenetical undergraduates took it upon themselves to occupy the local Army Recruiting Headquarters by way of protest. The University authorities should have "sent down" the offenders on the instant, but it is improbable that any kind of disciplinary action was taken against them. Much emphasis is placed on "academic freedom", but to allow universities to become hot beds of subversion forms no part of that freedom and a healthy society would take drastic steps to stop the rot.

In the latest instance cited there is some semblance of an excuse for the errant Oxford cubs in that, with the exception of Mr. Paget and one or two other known patriots in their ranks, the parliamentary Labour Party flung themselves with joyous abandon into an orgy of denunciation of Britain's elite Parachute Regiment. The shooting and bombing of British soldiers these same screaming gentlemen had accepted with the stiff upper-lip traditionally associated with British stoicism!

It will be said of the undergraduates, what cannot be said of Labour M.P.s., that only a very small proportion of them are responsible for such attitudes and demonstrations. This is incontestable. The majority are no doubt very pleasant young people who in their private lives do their utmost to uphold the human decencies. My criticism of them, as of my fellow-countrymen as a whole, is that they allow enemies to dominate their institutions and set the general tone of modern society. They are unaware of the extent to which their sins of omission endanger the future of the Western World.

The need for student majority action is all the greater because of the success achieved by those who activate the militant minority and who are able to secure key posts on university staffs. Political motivation is exposed whenever student unrest erupts, as happened at Lancaster. An exterior Board of Examiners had expressed concern at the evidence of political indoctrination revealed in papers submitted by students in the English Department and had also drawn attention to the alleged favouritism shown by internal examiners towards those whose views were congenial to their own. The first charge was answered, not very convincingly, by the argument that it was natural for a strong teacher so to impress his personality on students that there resulted a uniformity of opinion, while the second charge was denied.

Anxious to put matters right, the Vice-Chancellor directed that Dr. David Craig, senior lecturer in English and a member of the internal Board of Examiners, should devote his energies to another aspect of the Department's work. This decision was not well received by the students, who organised protest demonstrations leading to undisciplined conduct and a boycott of lectures. At the start of the next term the Vice-Chancellor stipulated that students sign a promise of good behaviour on pain of not receiving their grants.

The response of the dissident students, about 1,500 in number, was to defer the boycott campaign and substitute rent strikes by those in residence. Strangely, the university — dropping the requirement of good behaviour pledges — proclaims that a victory for discipline had been *won,* which called forth further protests. There were demands that the motion before the Council to dismiss Dr. Craig be withdrawn, supported by a one-day strike by forty members of the Association of Technical, Scientific and Managerial staffs.

Who was the Dr. Craig at the centre of all the storm and stress? A card-carrying Communist. Is it possible for university life to be carried on in an atmosphere of open rebellion and strife? Surely not. But unless the same elements drop this non-involvement and become very deeply involved the whole structure of higher education must be brought crashing to the ground. That is what the subversives most ardently desire — but not for the benefit of British youth.

Chapter 5

# ANARCHY IN THE SCHOOLS

It was to have been expected that the movement to encourage subversion in the universities would soon be extended to the schools. The ground had been prepared, not only by the "free discipline" establishments pioneered by men such as A. S. Neill who (often on their own showing) produced batches of little horrors, but also by the latterday public schools, with the once elite Eton in the vanguard. In the 'sixties, for instance, Dr. Robert Birley, then Headmaster of Eton, announced a prize essay competition on a subject embracing racial integration — a matter which all races proud of their identity regard with loathing. Asked to judge the essays was the notorious integrationist, negrophile and anti-patriot — now ennobled --- Lord Fenner Brockway. In the circumstances it was not surprising that every entrant had been enthusiastically in favour of the integrationist cause. Indoctrination at Eton must have been thorough!

During the last two decades the relaxing of discipline in almost every public school has been continuous. Following the ludicrous attempt to establish Student Power, no less nonsensical concepts such as Sixth Form Power were heard in establishments all over the country, and, where headmasters had been infected with the liberal disease, efforts were often made to give effect to them. This led some of us to ask sardonically: Why not Lower Fourth Power? Why not Power for the Embryo? The first of these questions was soon answered.

The chief function and main justification of the public schools were that they turned out not only scholars but leaders, and that even when these ends were not achieved the system imparted to all who had been subjected to it a sense of loyalty, decency and social discipline. Where today are we to look with any assurance for these qualities in the nation's youth? Included in the sense of decency was, above all, a passion for fair play, not only in games but over the entire spectrum of life. What fair play had been manifested in those masters who made integrationists of the Eton schoolboys? What steps had they taken to demonstrate to them the cruelty and misery of miscegenation? Obviously, none.

I have been hearing of a South African schoolmaster who, under some exchange system, found himself teaching at Wellington College in England. He happens to be a man with exceptional fondness for factual accuracy and he was astonished, dismayed and almost driven up the wall when he listened to diatribes by his charges about White oppression, apartheid and general conditions in Southern Africa —diatribes unsupported by a single fact or by any knowledge whatever of the enormous sociological and geo-political problems which South Africans have to face. This disgraceful ignorance was not the fault of the boys, but of the mentors who had unscrupulously fed them with left-wing, liberal propaganda masquerading as knowledge. What makes this experience the more painful was the school where it had been encountered. Wellington College was founded for the education of sons of Army officers and to some extent it still fills this role. If the lack of fair play in the instruction given by some of its masters is manifest at Wellington, what hope is there of finding honest teaching in the country's comprehensive and secondary schools? What hope, indeed, is there of finding the enforcement of normal discipline?

Over the whole field of education unruliness is paving the way for anarchy. Many readers will be shocked when they read the facts that follow. They are a summary of the views of Mr. Terry Casey, general-secretary of the National Association of Schoolmasters. In two months more than 200 well-documented cases of violence and vandalism by play-ground thugs were contributed by the members of this relatively small body to a dossier sent to the Government. It showed that more and more time was being wasted in the sheer rudiments of keeping order and less and less on teaching. Too many local education chiefs and teachers were trying to hush things up. "We are going down the road towards a situation now existing in New York where they have policemen in the classroom."

Mr. Casey gives the following examples of gangsterdom: The recent stabbing of a 14-year-old boy prompted notice of questions in the House of Commons, a 16-year-old Strand grammar school pupil told how he was threatened with a knife by a gang from nearby Tulse Hill Comprehensive School, six boys at a secondary school in South London repeatedly tried to start fires during lessons. All hurled abuse at teachers. One assaulted a woman teacher. Two threw a chair through a window. All terrorised classmates and one threatened a teacher with a knife. In South West London a primary school head-master clipped the ear of a boy during an incident involving 100 pupils. The boy's elder brother came to the school brandishing a club and broke the head's nose. In Birmingham a secondary school teacher was repeatedly abused by a boy he found out of bounds. Eventually the boy kicked him in the groin. The teacher chased and tackled the still fighting boy, finally hitting him on the jaw. Legal action was taken — against the teacher! Fortunately he was tried by a judge and and jury, which acquitted him, the judge remarking that we were "living in strange times" and asking — "Have we really reached the stage in schools in this country where an insolent and bolshie pupil was to be treated with all the courtesies of visiting royalty?" In Stoke a headmaster wanted to suspend two boys for persistent bad behaviour. Directors of the school refused. Now the boys go around giving the "V" sign to the staff. In the East Midlands school prefects in the fifth and sixth form were beaten up by gangs of younger boys. In Preston a teacher was kicked in the face, nearly losing his eyesight, when attempting to stop a fight at a youth club attached to the school.

Horrifying though these examples are, we must remember that they represent only a small segment in the general pattern of schoolboy violence. As Mr. Casey says, too many educational authorities and teachers are much more concerned in hushing up these matters than in making the nation aware of the growing dangers attendant upon school life. Although the young hoodlums are not free from blame (most of us are very well aware of what should be meted out to them) the heavier responsibility rests with those teachers who lack the guts to get to grips with them, and the heaviest responsibility of all must be placed upon the timid educational authorities who seek to restrain the teachers from taking appropriate measures.

A boy at a Croydon School led his schoolmates, boys and girls, in unruly behaviour which resulted in their being "kept in". While in detention, he again led them into misbehaviour. They wrote obscene essays. Thereupon the senior mistress gave each girl a cut with a cane on the hand, and the headmaster did the same to the boys. When the ringleader's turn came, however, he refused to accept the punishment. Older generations may remember what would have happened to them had they dared to take so insubordinate a stance. All that happened to this young worthy was that the Head allowed him to leave the school premises, with the warning that he would not be permitted to return until he agreed to be caned.

The national newspapers seized hold of the story, which they "splashed", while the ever-enterprising B.B.C. secured a television interview with the boy—his age, I think, was 13 or thereabouts—and treated him with profound respect. He became something of a national hero. Meanwhile in Croydon the "crisis" mounted. Backed by his school-managers, the Headmaster reaffirmed that on no account would he receive the boy back at school until he had apologised and submitted his palm for a stroke of the cane. The Education Committee of the Croydon Borough Council met, spent a long time deliberating the weighty issue and finally announced that the boy should be permitted to return without being caned, as he had been punished enough by being barred. Misconduct, it seems, pays off! One of the school-managers began to waver, and then the Headmaster, jovially eating his own words, declared that he would be delighted to welcome the young gentleman back with open arms, adding that he bore him no malice and hoped that the boy bore him none either. At this point, it so happened, some wishy-washy do-gooders who ran a fee-paying school, wishing to show sympathy with the charming little martyr, offered to educate him without fee. The offer was accepted and the "crisis" thereby resolved.

There could be no better example of the state of education in Britain today than this ignoble farce. Not one single actor failed to show, in one way or another, the liberal sickness which is destroying our national will to survive. No wonder a situation is being reached wherein it can be predicted that the schoolmaster will soon require to have policemen in his class to keep order which he himself either cannot or is not allowed to keep.

Chapter 6

# AMOK-RUN OF THE SEXOLOGISTS

We saw something in the last chapter of the interactions between the teachers and the taught. Here we shall consider the pressure brought to bear upon youth from outside by influences which, whether or not malign in intention, cannot fail to undermine and deprave.

Despite the fact that the Council of Civil Liberties is orientated far to the Left— I recall no instance where it has intervened on behalf of the oppressed Right— the Establishment regards it as a responsible body, worthy of respect. Here is a report which recently appeared in the *Guardian*: " 'Young children should have the right to sexual relations as soon as they wish to', the Children's Committee of the National Council of Civil Liberties said yesterday. In a document entitled 'Children have Rights' the Committee says 'The right of young people to have sexual relations as soon as they wish to have them is a most important one, and of course carries with it the right to contraceptive information, advice and equipment'. The Committee says 'it is unfortunate for children to live in housing conditions which do not allow privacy for such activity'. 'All the talk about increasing sexual freedom comes to naught without opportunity for some privacy in the home. To compel a child to leave home, perhaps to attend boarding school, is an infringement of civil liberty'."

It is impossible to think of a more reckless or deplorable proposition. Society, it seems, is to find the money to pay birth-control experts to give information and advice, and to present contraceptives, to young boys from the age of fourteen — for what grand purpose? That they should arrive at adulthood sated and exhausted, deprived forever of the wonder and beauty and mystery of a stable sexual relationship? How surprisingly fastidious of the Civil Liberties Committee to desire privacy for such juvenile "love"-making! Perhaps legislation will soon require all residences to have annexes with the notice: "Parents Keep Out". As for those benighted parents who send their sons and daughters to boarding school, the day may come when they appear before international courts charged with crimes against juvenile humanity! That early sex could be a potent weapon in debilitating a nation's youth, with the ultimate object of weakening the nation by depriving it of any power of manly resistance, is all too probable. Hence, perhaps, the toleration of its vendors.

Even overseas readers are likely to have heard of the egregious Dr. Cole, who caused a furore in the English Midlands by producing what is said to be a very bad film called "Growing Up". It was intended to be shown in schools for the purpose of providing visible sex instruction. Dr. Cole was not prosecuted, but one of his helpers, a young woman teacher, lost her job. Her amiable part in the film was to give a physical demonstration of a girl masturbating. When she met with official displeasure and lost her job she became furious. "After all", she exclaimed, "it was purely (sic) a private matter." Had it been a "public matter" I wonder in what other ways she would have consented to be filmed. Should that be irrelevant, one would at least like to know how she would differentiate between "private" and "public". Whatever the answer, it is worth recording that, the liberal sickness being as virulent in the Midlands as anywhere, the authorities had second thoughts, decided that after all the young woman was suited to have educational responsibility and duly reinstated her as a teacher. Her mentor, Dr. Cole, is still traipsing round the country with his obsession.

Then there was the case of the pornographic magazine *Oz*, intended to be seen and read by adults, albeit adults who retain the pimply mind of the retarded adolescent. The editors of this choice publication, in a bid to extend the range of its readership, decided to bring out a "School Kids' Edition". Accordingly, they began to collect muck written and drawn by the smuttiest-minded juveniles who could be fished out of the cess-pools. The result was such that not even the Public Prosecutor could fail to take action. Orders were given for the arrest of the unsavoury editorial gang, of whom the leading spirit was a 34-year-old barrister who would not have needed to practise beneath a judicial wig as his greasy locks, like those of his colleagues, extended halfway down his back. Remanded in custody, something then happened to them which sent the entire left-wing in Britain into a hysterical frenzy. The Prison officials had their gorgeous tresses cut off. It is impossible to exaggerate the shrieks of outrage when this hygienic act became known to the outside world. (Unless I am mistaken, the Home Office, ever anxious to appease the rabble, was quick to issue a directive that in future the hair of prisoners on remand must be treated as sacrosanct.)

The lock-shearing was only the prologue to the swelling theme. Twenty years ago no part of the Yellow Press would have been yellow enough to treat the *Oz* obscenities with anything but loathing. But times change, and with them *The Times*, reputed to be the country's leading newspaper, but now prepared, it would seem, to make the vivid yellow press look demure. The brashest of its columnists, crinkly-haired Mr. Bernard Levin, was allowed to go to town on the *Oz* case. He addressed himself with a will to the cause of the Abominable Smutmen and delivered a savage attack on the judge who passed sentence on them. There is nothing Master Levin does not know. (Although he has been around for 20 years or more one still thinks of him as a Lower Fourth essayist.) Raise what questions you will, he is there to pronounce the final word on it. He described the *Oz* trial as "a national disgrace". After quoting a sentence which had appeared in *The Times* six months earlier which read: "*The young look at their father's world and see that much of what they say is bogus*", Levin added his own explosive comment.

"By God they do, too. Dimly, they recognise what lies at the root of sexual repression is commonly repressed sexual envy. That one of the drawings in the School Kids' *Oz* depicted a middle-aged teacher manipulating his own penis with one hand and a schoolboy's buttocks with the other is not a coincidence— and it is not obscene, either. It is a defiant statement that if it is all right for the children's fathers to tell jokes about the barmaid and the commercial traveller it should be all right for the children to feel sexual desire, and even express it, without their fathers calling the police." It can be said in honesty that never in my life have I read such atrocious nonsense. That last analogy is bereft of all meaning, while it would indeed be a gifted reader who managed to track the line of thought between that middle-aged teacher's foul activity and "Sexual envy". Moreover, if such a drawing is not pornographic it is a merciful dispensation of Providence that one is not able to delve into the Levin mind to discover what he considers would warrant that description.

Levin himself is of no account in the national scheme of things, but the same cannot be said of *The Times*, at any rate as long as it retains the reputation, however misplaced, of being the authoritative voice of the British people. While the comment quoted is unlikely to have any effect on children, the filth produced in *Oz* by them and for them must assuredly rub off on those who are brought into contact with it. Defilement of Britain's youth is a rapidly expanding process that conforms with the general pattern of national degeneration at all levels, which is both reflected and furthered by contemporary literature, the baser kind of newspaper, the more ignoble clergy (including some at the top of the hierarchy), the so-called "intellectuals", the theatre, the cinema and, above all, B.B.C. television. That the most brazen and disgusting attempt to corrupt young boys and girls yet made in Britain, the vileness of the *Oz* publication, should receive *The Times* newspaper's cachet of approval surely registers the lowest water-mark ever reached in the British annals of public indecency.

The writer of this denunciation is a soldier of the two World Wars and as a journalist and author often has had to report on matters revealing human degradation. I think it improbable that any form of words or pictorial delineation now has power to shock me. What I do find shocking beyond all adequate means of expression is the use of these devices to contaminate children or naive adults' minds, thereby debasing to sewer-level the standards of private and public life. My anger increases when I suspect the bestiality to be under any kind of official protection. I gave one such example early in this book. Another was the recent experience of a Mr. Knapman, who withdrew his young daughter from a school where homosexuality and masturbation were being extolled in the class-room. He was brought before a Court and sentenced to pay a fine for his "offence". Whether that magistrate was following a Home Office or Ministry of Education directive I do not know. If he was, then something very much more important than one magistrate's aberration is obviously at issue.

What brings my anger to white heat is the knowledge that the climate of opinion in which it is possible for the degenerative process to work has been induced by evil subterranean influences intent upon destroying not only our own brave old country but the Western civilisation which it has done so much to help to build. Before probing beneath the surface to examine these influences, we should look at some of the end products, or what may prove to be the end products, of the depraved trends we have so far studied.

# Chapter 7

# HIPPIES AND SQUARES

After the last war some young men took up the business, generally quite honest, of selling fruit, vegetables and other merchandise in the streets. For a reason unknown to me—could it have been the resentment of shopkeepers? — they were called "Barrow-Boys", a term carrying with it public scorn. When they faded out they were replaced by "Teddy-Boys", young worthies whose dress vaguely recalled that of the Edwardian era. They, too, met with the derision of their elders. I do not aspire to be an historian of these cults and my chronology may be wrong, but as far as I can remember the "Teds" were succeeded by two warring sets called "Mods" and "Rockers", whose favourite sport was to converge on seaside resorts at weekends, fight each other, assault holiday-makers and attack the police, who had special squads standing by, ready to be taken by helicopter to any scene of trouble.

By this time youth had long since became enamoured of long hair, face fungus and jeans. When walking in the wake of any couple it was (and remains) impossible from the back to distinguish male from female—not that it mattered! Then the terms "mods" and "rockers" became obsolescent and the word "hippies" was pushed into general use to embrace all the long-haired clans. The opposition movement took the form of young men of ferocious disposition who cut their hair short and made their forays on motor-cycles to beat up hippies and anybody else who might serve as target. They were and are a pretty brutal crowd.

The hippies, although distasteful to the eye, tend on the whole to be non-aggressive in conduct. It was they, unless I am mistaken, who bred a sub-species called the Flower-Folk, whose favourite slogan, often enough, was: "Make Love, Not War". This idea seems to be approved by the hippy population as a whole. Not long ago—by kind permission of the Duke of Bedford—several thousands of them swarmed into the ground of Woburn Abbey, many equipped with sleeping-bags for two, for what they called a "love-in", described by others as a "group-grope". It is curious, and perhaps significant, that whatever these youngsters do nowadays they find essential to do gregariously. Perhaps *au fonde*, they lack self-confidence.

It is this vast hippy population that gives the commercially-minded the opportunity to cash in — using that term literally — for their support. Carnaby Street and discotheques throughout the country indeed all over the Western world make fortunes out of the cult. So do the organisers of Pop Festivals. Nearly two hundred thousand hippies attended one such occasion in the Isle of Wight. In the year 1972 there was a proposal to hold another on the mainland which half a million were expected to attend. The residents near the site chosen, fearful of the noise and the laying-waste of vast tracts of countryside, successfully protested, but the organisers were confident of being able to find another site in time for their summer Festival. Half a million hippies congregated at the same place!

Friends of mine on the Isle of Wight told me that many of the hippy visitors whom they encountered seemed amiable and polite young people, which I can quite believe. Never the less it is astounding to me that half a million of them (and probably many more) should be happy to put up with the discomfort of forming part of a huge crowd, primitive eating and sleeping conditions and a constant jostling, simply to hear music derived from the jungle and to scream hysterically with the mounting excitement of the "beat". The "generation-gap", they tell me, accounts for my detestation of the music, which is as it may be. But the screaming, the hysteria, the extraordinary mass emotional response — it is difficult to believe that what separates the older generations from sympathy and understanding of such things is merely a matter of years. We did not lack sympathetic, understanding of our grandfathers' generation and I do not recollect that their generation lacked sympathetic understanding of ours. But today! It does really seem that a totally different kind of human being has been born and somehow bred.

The difference lies not only in taste and activity, but even more in appearance. If they had the slightest idea of the impression they make it is just possible they might be less ready to display themselves. As it is, they reveal a passionate desire to take part in demonstration marches. Any occasion will do as long as it is left-inclined. One watches incredulously as what seems miles of them march — more accurately shuffle — through the streets of London or wherever it may be. Hair at shoulder length (as the minimum), weak eyes discernible in the middle of faces fringed with unkempt wisps of beard, dirty jeans and sometimes esoteric ornamentation around the neck, they shuffle along behind placards and from time to time thrust clenched fists aloft — fists so pathetic that they could scarcely knock down a stuffed dummy.

Those of us who are apparently on the wrong side of the age gap — as well, I suspect, as foreign visitors — can only ask "Are these really British men and women? Indeed, are they really human beings?" Their appearance suggests a weird emanation of the bogs in some Nightmareland remote from earth. How any "leader" can think that he does other than grave disservice to his "cause" by staging such freakish displays is inexplicable.

Demonstrations of this kind sometimes lead to disorder and give extra work and annoyance to the police, but they are not of themselves a social menace. The idea of menace occurs only when we remember how tough and dangerous is the world we inhabit, and begin to wonder how our needs, and those of countries similarly afflicted, can be met when so large a proportion of youth exults in showing itself in public as all too visible symptoms of the liberal sickness — as symbols, indeed, of civilisation in decay. The paradox is that today their own world should be threatened by Skinheads, Greasers, Hell's Angels, call them what you may whose will to cruelty is excited by the effeminate Hippies and whose aggression may drive them from the streets.

There are associated problems. Many hippies no doubt come to terms with life, marry and settle down as responsible citizens. Where this happens, it does so, not as the end to which hippydom directs them, but as a reaction against the main hippy trend. In the long-haired realm of unisex (a word I do not know how to define, but which I take to mean that the heterosexual and the homosexual require no differentiation — everything "goes") the big idea is liberation from all disciplines and restraints and social taboos, which often means an encouragement to explore avenues that the wisdom of the ages has found better left unexplored.

How many young heterosexuals have been won over to homosexuality in this permissive atmosphere there is no means of knowing, but complaints made by horrified parents are not infrequently heard. That there is an even closer association of a certain kind of hippy with drug-taking is more easily demonstrated. For some years in Cape Town, during my annual visits, office-facilities were available to me next door to a hippy "joint". I watched them go by from time to time and wondered at their constant change of expression, exultation one day turning to surly depression the next, and then the swift return to contentment. There was no doubt in my mind as to the cause and therefore no surprise when the Narcotics Squad went there one night and made forty arrests. This is only one small example.

It would be absurd and most unfair to imagine that every "bearded-weirdie" is a "pot" or LSD addict: most of them clearly are not, otherwise the problem would be insoluble. Nevertheless, that drug-taking is one of the hippy manifestations today cannot be denied. Moreover, unfortunately for the British name, the nomads among them tend to travel eastwards, almost certainly to be nearer the sources of supply, and they turn up in lands where once the British name was honoured.

Afghanistan, for example is one of the biggest drug-producing countries. The smug hippy types and their mentors in the "intellectual" world sneer prodigiously at the British Raj, but the Afghans had a very healthy respect for Tommy Atkins as he kept watch and word over the Khyber Pass to prevent their descent into India to murder, rape and rob the adjacent population. It may be that the B.B.C. and all the other decriers of the British Empire prefer the picture of many Britons in the East today which I am about to relate.

Mr. Peter Wiley, a master of Wellington College, was awarded a Churchill Scholarship wherewith to go to Afghanistan to study the life and works of an eleventh century poet. When he arrived he was appalled by what he found. In a report to the Anti-Slavery Society he told of "British" hippies "living" in squares that reek of death and decay. "They have become dependent on scraps of food, contemptuous charity and a daily supply of hashish or other narcotics provided by Afghans who treat them as weird human pets. These young men will sell their possessions, their bodies and those of their girl friends to buy their hash." Is Broadcasting House happier with this picture than that of "pukkha sahibs in Poona?" I would not be surprised.

The deplorable situation in Kandahar as described by Mr. Wiley has its counterpart in Katmandu and other Eastern cities. So general did the problem of British and American hippies become in India that Delhi felt obliged to take special steps to deal with it. The Singapore Government, accurately associating conduct of the kind just described with hippydom, will not allow any male with hair below his collar to sleep a single night in Singapore, even as a passenger in transit. The final shame was the decree of Jomo Kenyatta, "leader to darkness and death" forbidding these creatures entry into Kenya.

It will be objected that all British youth is not long-haired, that those who do grow their hair long are not necessarily hippies, and that few hippies become drop-outs at home or get washed up as flotsam and jetsam on some foreign strand, to turn up for the curious pleasure of Afghan gentlemen.

The objection is valid, but it does not conceal the fact that British youth has now mostly become identified by the public with hippydom or the further fact that youthful thinking (for want of a better word) is being largely influenced by what passes for thought in the hippy mind. The very nearly all-prevailing attitude is that youth does not like the world it has inherited from its parents and that by kicking over the traces it can wrest that world from the hands of the "squares" and build it anew, upon specifications unlikely to get beyond the jargon stage but nevertheless hopefully ensuring freedom from any kind of restraint. But what restraints are there still to be removed? Let them ask it — the world they despise does not have it. Do they want pornography? Soho and the cinemas are tumbling over each other to meet their wants and the B.B.C., to add good measure, shows them the judge's daughter enjoying the carnal attentions of the village idiot on the lawn — with three close-ups too, so as not to be taunted with over-refinement! Do they want to deviate and for their deviation to be recognised, perhaps even honoured? Why was the Rev. Hugh Montefiore made Suffragan Bishop of Kingston-on-Thames after he had said that Jesus could have been a homosexual? Did not His Grace of Canterbury vote *for* homosexuality among consenting adults and *against* an amendment which would have excluded sodomy? So go to it, Christian deviates! Do they want instant sadism? They have but to prowl around the bookshops for almost any modern novel or press one or other of the buttons on their sets and they will find cruelty and violence to suit all tastes. Have they an urge to play bumpsadaisy with all other colours and shades of colour? To meet that urge, good, kind, considerate Conservative and Labour Governments have filled the land with every colour and every shade of colour that has ever graced the human skin. Have they not cause for gratitude and joy?

The one question they are not likely to ask is this: What is wrong with themselves — the rebellious, frenetical brats who have reached adulthood with all the spoilt child inside them left intact? I give the answer. It is that the parental "squares" against whom they go through the motions of rebelling have not enough shape to them to form any kind of geometrical figure. Had they as parents some dimension, some will, some sense of what constitutes the dignity of man then their offspring would not roam the streets today looking like abortions which some black magic had disastrously managed to keep alive. They would step the streets like men and women with pride of bearing and proud of their own kind, its historic past, its aspiring present and splendid future destiny. Writing this, alas, does not give shape to the bogus squares or a sense of purpose to the nation's youth.

Chapter 8

# THE CONDITIONING PROCESS

Thus far we have considered symptoms rather than causes of the liberal disease which has stricken Great Britain and the West. In the fields covered by the preceding chapters it has been impossible to draw a line between conspiratorial and non-conspiratorial influences at work. There are, however, some pointers. Nothing is less likely than that Cohn-Bendit and his rather dim-witted followers paid the expenses of their various campaigns out of their own pocket. The question arises — who did? Obviously possessors of wealth who had a direct interest in subversion and the fomenting of riots.

Another pointer is that, underlying local grievances in the universities throughout the West, there has been a central motif. The language of subversion spoken by the initiates never varies — it is anti-patriotic, anti-racial differentiation and hostile to all national values and traditions. Almost always Chairs of Sociology go to professors associated or known to be in harmony with one or other of the various Race-Relations agencies preaching the unnatural doctrine of racial integration. These appointments are much too constant to be fortuitous: they are part of the plan to destroy Western civilisation and replace it with a One World order in which an elite few will control the masses conditioned to obey.

As yet in Britain and the Western European countries, we have seen only the destroyers at work. The United States of America, having been brought nearer to social breakdown and its resultant chaos, affords glimpses of the techniques of creating the anything but brave new world wherein human beings are to be given a status not dissimilar from that of ants.

At the time this book is being written Professor B. F. Skinner of Harvard holds the stage. The importance attached to him and his views may be judged by the attack made by former Vice-President Agnew, who called him "a serious threat to liberty, a planner whose sugar-coated theories treat man not as an individual but as one of a herd". It is Skinner's view, set out at length in a book *Beyond Freedom and Dignity*, that individual freedom is a delusion and that human behaviour must be made to conform to the best interests of society by a system of psychological controls. As one critic has put it, the book is "a blue-print for a

State which uses the resources of science to condition the behaviour of its citizens".

Before the reader decides to disregard the "blueprint" as the outpourings of a crank, let him consider one remarkable fact which has astounded Congress — for the research and writing of this book the United States Government made a grant of £100,000 and subsequent approval was forthcoming when *Beyond Freedom and Dignity* won a handsome prize awarded by the Joseph P. Kennedy Foundation. This disclosure led Congressman Cornelius Gallacher, in the van of a Congressional move to have the whole matter investigated, to the discovery that Skinner's influence is pervasive and that many American schools are already practising his methods. He found, moreover, after a careful search of official documents, that "tens of thousands" of other behavioural research projects have been launched by bodies such as the Pentagon and the Departments of Labour and Education.

Those who deride the conspiratorial theory are no doubt dwelling on the happy accidents which brought together Skinner, the United States Government and the Joseph P. Kennedy Foundation, and the joyous coincidences that a vast number of similar research projects have been put in hand by official U.S. bodies. To do that is to be more than a little credulous. That the conditioning of man is very much in the forefront of the minds behind the American scenes can be deduced by other methods which their scientists and educationists are putting forward to attain the same ends. For example, a negro psychologist well-known in the United States — his name is Kenneth Clark— recently wrote that religion, moral philosophy, law and education are no longer appropriate in modern society and suggested "psychotechnological medication", especially the giving of drugs to stimulate certain areas of the brain. Does it not seem that the Devil himself is taking charge of the human race?

Let us pursue this theme a little further. Dr. Reginald Lourse is reported by Jeremy Campbell, the brilliant correspondent in Washington of the *Evening Standard*, to have told Congress: "There is serious thinking among researchers that perhaps we cannot trust the family alone to prepare young children for the new kind of world which is emerging. This is why the Soviets feel they need access to infants. Remember that the brain grows fastest in the first 18 months of life. It is more plastic for appropriate experience and corrective intervention." Who is this would-be emulator of the Soviets? Dr. Lourse is President of a U.S. commission on the mental health of young children. Professor Skinner agrees.

"The family is now failing", he declares. "I think we are going to have experimental communities in this country".

Former Vice-President Agnew, in his speech attacking Skinner, revealed what is even today taking place in American schools. Children are being made to perform psychodramas in the classroom, acting out scenes in which they obtain an abortion, smoke marijuana and practise inter-racial dating. "School counsellors have been meeting with small groups of children," Agnew said, "and asking such questions as 'What does your father wear when he shaves?' Do you love your parents?' One child was assigned to write an essay on the subject 'Why do I hate my mother more than my father?'"

Britons who shrug off the thought of these horrors as being "American" and therefore remote from our own shores are profoundly mistaken. The breaking-down process is at work on every level of our national life and all that happens is not coincidental, any more than the attempts at mental conditioning, and psychological slavery in the United States are coincidental. The planners are busy, no less so because, like the late Bernard Baruch, they are "fighters in the long grass".

I have heard it suggested that one means of conditioning the mind is what has become known as "psychedelic music". When The Beatles first made their bow, although I abominated the sounds they made — that generation-gap again! — it seemed to me that they were four decent young Liverpudlians who had a gift which appealed to their contemporaries, were surprised at their success and wore it with becoming modesty. Whatever their subsequent history, I think that first impression of mine was right at the time I formed it and I am convinced that the boys were not then, and have not since become, conscious agents of an assault upon civilisational values.

Having said that, I quote from *Behind the News*, edited by my friend Ivor Benson, South Africa's best-informed and most brilliant journalist:

"'Psychedelic music as inspired by the pop group The Beatles represents a serious attack on youth, church and state and is an influence generated directly by Communism,' writes Dr. H. G. van der Hoven, in the latest issue of *Kerkbode*, official organ of the Nederduitse Gereformeerde Kerk. He goes on: `It has been mentioned that this cruel and satanic assault stems from a thorough scientific background resulting from research done by Pavlov, Lauria, and Platinov. We have to deal here with an aspect of the Cold War and this method is an excellent example of the so-called psychological warfare which is aimed at injuring our children's minds. This music is definitely claiming victims in South Africa and our Church by conveying the message that God is dead. It also presents Christ as a homosexual, as a person who lived in sin with Mary Magdalene as presented in Jesus Christ Superstar'."

While still maintaining my stance about the personal motivation of The Beatles, I cannot gainsay what this passage conveys about the shock-effect of the battery upon the senses, although until recently I would not have recognised its truth. It so happens that two or three years ago the undergraduate son of some close friends of mine—he specialises in electronics —took us to his den to hear "music" that had been electronically contrived. It was clear to me that his own interest in the matter was solely technological, but as the sounds came forth the thought formed in my mind: "This thing is evil". A few moments later I had heard enough. "This thing is positively diabolical", I told myself.

So it may be (although they themselves would never recognise, let alone admit, the possibility) that the scores of thousands of frenzied youngsters who jump around screaming at pop-festivals come under some kind of demonic control. Nevertheless, how Dr. van der Hoven traces the evil to Moscow is not clear, and neither is the Pavlovian influence. I do not deny that the evil is motivated but having a fondness for hard facts neither can I confirm its motivation. Psychedelic "music" obviously has an adverse effect on those subjected to it, obliterating their dignity and very often, it would seem, destroying their self-respect.

Another matter, more compact and therefore easier to assess, was the Holy Communion service in St. Paul's Cathedral to celebrate the third anniversary of the musical show *Hair*. This was something completely out of the ordinary, even in the lesser context of a commercial concern being boosted by the Church of England — and boosted in one of the country's two most famous places of worship. The play, I am told, has some pleasing ballet, but it is not the dancing which has made its name known to the public or, as I suspect, commended it to the dignitaries entrusted with the running of St. Paul's. No, the interest lies in the scene wherein the entire cast, men and women, take off all their clothes and go gallumping round the stage stark naked. Personally, I can imagine no sight less attractive, but the Dean and Chapter of St. Paul's must think otherwise. The question of motive arises. Wrote a commentator of the *Daily Telegraph*: "It is not surprising that those who are fighting drug addiction, obscenity, blasphemy and the contemporary obsession with sex should manifest something like despair at the near-canonisation of the cast of *Hair* involving the holding of a special communion service for them at St. Paul's." As this was the normal Christian reaction, one has to search for the motive which emboldened the Church functionaries to affront their followers.

Was it simply that broad-minded churchmen, aware of a falling-off in attendance, were making a desperate attempt to capture youth by showing how much "with it" they were? Or has the answer to be sought at some deeper level? One remembers the other "causes" with which St. Paul's has been associated in recent years. Canon Collins, one of its functionaries, took a leading part in the Campaign for Nuclear Disarmament, the result of which — if successful — would leave Britain completely disarmed in a nuclear-armed world. The same worthy gentleman seemed to make a point, on every available occasion, of identifying himself with any movement directed against his own countrymen overseas, which in fact meant championing the cause of barbarism in revolt against civilised government, although that is not how he himself would see it. Some years ago I was invited by Western Television to take part in a programme on St. George's Day. Arriving at the Plymouth studio, I was surprised to find Canon Collins on the same panel. I wondered what he would have to say in praise of Englishry on this patriotic occasion. I am still left wondering.

In the wider Church context we mentioned the backing the Archbishop of Canterbury gave to the bill legalizing homosexuality among consenting adults and his disapproval of an amendment which sought to exempt sodomy. Among all the nationally-known clerics in Great Britain we cannot think of one who stands forth as an opponent of the liberal, leftward trend. Nor is there much light observable on the international horizon. The World Council of Churches, dominated by the same sick influences as those active in Britain, has provided funds to sustain terrorists rebelling against Portuguese rule in Angola and Mozambique. When such patronage ran into a storm of protest the Council's spokesmen defended the granting of aid on the ground that an assurance was required of the terrorists' leadership that on no account would the monies made available be used for the purchase of arms. The naivete (if such it was) which accepted such an assurance from unscrupulous desperados is beyond belief. Even if the word of the rebel leaders could be trusted, it must have been obvious to the Council's officials that monies supplied for food and clothing would have released monies otherwise used for these needs to be switched to the purchase of arms. The explanation of naivete must therefore be ruled out. There is no reasonable doubt that the World Council of Churches serves as an outwardly respectable and "spiritual" front for the under-mining of Western civilisation — beginning, as Lenin declared to be necessary, on its peripheries.

Not, of course, as we have seen that the attack is confined to far-off issues. When the Reverend Hugh Montefiore (the Sebag Montefiores are related to the Rothschilds) declared that Christ might have been a homosexual, so far from blotting his copybook with the Church of England, he was swiftly made Suffragan Bishop of Kingston-on-Thames. Father Huddleston, who had worked more than his stint on trying to overthrow civilised government in South Africa, was rewarded with the Bishopric of Stepney. By blinding his eyes to the reality of barbarism wearing a synthetic cloak of sophistication, Huddleston no doubt felt that he was upholding Christian values, without having the slightest realisation that in fact he was helping to destroy them. Is there in the public eye today a single cleric whose activities have not been gravely injurious to Christianity?

Thus far we have seen two major influences at work -- that which seeks to lay waste our traditional society, for the most part through exploiting the immaturity of youth, and that which has begun the task of conditioning the young to inhabit the ant-like world projected by the would-be masters of mankind. When youth is asked why it allows its mind to be inflamed we are told that it does not like the world which it inherits and wants something better — the dream of men though all the ages.

The young, however, are too indoctrinated, too brain-washed by meaningless slogans, to understand that despite innumerable set-backs, the world through the ages has become a better, less barbarous place and that it can be improved, not by rejecting the past but by building upon what has already been achieved. Their own start upon creating a new society has not been attractive. What good is being served by nauseatingly long hair, feeble bits of face-fungus, outlandish garments, manners often abominable, useless violence, pop-music screaming and all the rest of it? Where are the leaders of their cult to be found, the pace-makers, the pioneers? In Kandahar?

The materialists who set such store on L.S.D. (in predecimal monetary terms) may often have been hypocritical in their lip-service to the things of the spirit, but at least they were not intent upon destroying the spirit. That cannot be said of the pedlars of L.S.D., who are the agents of Hell, as the Sharon Tate murders made clear. The drug-taking menace which is helping to encompass the ruin of the West is all too frequently overlooked, where indeed it is not actually encouraged. For instance, one of Britain's leading medical journals, *The Lancet*, which should have known better, some years ago advocated the legalization of the use of cannabis on the grounds that it was less dangerous than alcohol and tobacco. The sheer irresponsibility of such advocacy may be judged from the findings of the International Narcotics Control Board in its 1972 report. Although the Board mentioned the primacy of opium, morphine and heroin, "the most outstanding and dangerous of the drugs of abuse" in the illicit traffic, it gave a special warning about cannabis. I quote: "Reliable observations so far made show that the effects of cannabis consumption include variation in perception of time and place, disinhibition, dulling of attention, fragmentation of thought and an altered sense of identity". The present indications were that cannabis represented "a serious and growing danger in many countries, both in its inherent potential for harm and its association with other forms of drug abuse". It is to be hoped that the editor of *The Lancet* and the Members of Parliament who aspire to introduce legislation to legalize cannabis will heed this warning.

In general, the Board declared drug abuse in many countries has increased to become a "virtual epidemic", constituting a danger to public health and society. "Now it is universally acknowledged that this is a grave social malady and that its incidence, though varying in degree and charter from one country to another, is already world-wide and is still growing." Although small-time vendors may be used in the final stages of distribution, it is clear that the wholesale marketing is in the hands of the big-money boys. No doubt profit is the major inducement, but would it be farfetched to state that the deliberate helping forward of the decadence of the West could also be a factor in this wicked business?

In as far as the public had been led to believe that the real menace to society lies in the hard drugs, the true malignancy of the soft drugs deserves a chapter to itself.

Chapter 9

# THE CAPITALIST-COMMUNIST NEXUS

Thus far we have seen something of the influences at work to subvert the society handed down to us by our forefathers through hundreds of years of trial and effort. The emergent pattern has shown a steady trend towards ever more importance being attached to the individual — not the importance of individual monarchs, or individual barons, or individual plutocrats, but individual human beings. This process is in deadly danger in our own times of being thrown into reverse. As politics has become decreasingly the field of the amateur devoted to voluntary service and increasingly the domain of the professional, so has the Member of Parliament tended to become ever less an individual and ever more a cog in his party machine. The same thing is happening in industry and commerce. As more and more national monopolies are formed, and as more and more national monopolies are being turned into giant international monopolies, so everywhere is the "little man" being squeezed out and losing his independence. Nations are undergoing the same loss of sovereignty as the drive towards World Government proceeds apace. It follows that the larger the political area to be administered, the greater is the emphasis placed on standardization and the less is the tolerance of any form of opposition. We hear much about the collectivization of this or that activity and the benefits it is alleged to bring, but what the propagandists take care to hide is that collectivising farms, or whatever else, means in essence the collectivising of human beings.

It often happens that weak-minded people who have to be looked after for a time become institutionalized and prefer that state to freedom. The reader has been given some horrifying glimpses of attempts now being made in the United States to induce this attitude of mind in normal children from earliest infancy.

To fight such diabolism, to ensure that individual freedom now lost is regained and that no further inroads are made upon freedom, it is necessary to recognise two things — one, the liberal disease, and secondly, that one of the most fraudulent concepts ever propagated is the polarity of capitalism and communism. Marx wrote of the "contradictions" in the capitalist system, but here is the real "contradiction".

The first successful attack on Western Civilisation took place in October 1917, when the Russian Bolshevists overthrew the Menshevists and instituted the Union of Soviet Socialist Republics. Communism was not a modern phenomenon stemming from the Manifesto of 1848. From earliest times there have been people — primitive, it is true — who shared land, crops or flocks in common. Many still do. There have also been peoples, in the last century particularly, who sought to opt out of civilized society and establish their own little Utopias wherein the good life could be lived. Because of the human factor their duration was brief.

Lenin and Trotsky were the first men in history, however, who managed — with very strange backing — to replace a civilized order with one which purported to be Communist. I use the word "purported" because the regime was financed by large-scale subsidies from top banking-houses in New York, Hamburg and other centres of finance-capitalism and built up during its formative years by the industrial-capitalists of the Western world. Hence my warning about the fiction of polarity.

The part played by the partners of New York's Kuhn Loeb and Co. and their European affiliates in supplying Trotsky with funds is now too well known to need stressing here. What is less well known is the role of industrial-capitalism. Soon after the Revolution, when the Soviet economy was on the verge of total collapse, Lenin did not waste time in consulting the works of Karl Marx for a solution. Marxist economics, largely a rehash of the theories of Ricardo, have had about as much effect on the Soviet Union's development as have tracts issued by the Flat Earth Society in placing men on the moon. Instead, Lenin made an appeal to Bernard Baruch, the most powerful man in America, bidding him name his own price to reshape the economic life of Russia. While Baruch did not consider it expedient to accept the offer, there is some reason to think that he used his overwhelming influence to mobilise practical assistance. Very soon the Soviet Union became a hive of industry, but the industry was not indigenous: it came from afar.

A review of Anthony C. Sutton's study: *Western Technology and Soviet Economic Development, 1917 to 1930,* by the Canadian commentator Robert Klinck throws much light on what happened. So far from Russia's pulling herself up by her own boot-laces, as Communist propaganda would have us believe, almost all of the projects of the First Five Year Plan were designed by American companies. At least ninety-five per cent of the industrial structure received Western assistance, the agreement to grant concessions having been reached by the Russian Congress of Councils of the National Economy as early as December 1917.

A start was made with the Baku oil fields, which had gone out of production during the war. Massive quantities of equipment were supplied by the American firms of International Barnsdale Corporation and Lucey Manufacturing Corporation, supplemented by Hill Electrical Drills and Metropolitan Vickers (a British subsidiary of Westinghouse), to get production moving again and at a much faster rate. In 1927 General Electric entered the scene, by which time Norwegian, Italian, British and Japanese firms were also busy exploiting oil concessions in Russia. By 1930 there were nineteen large refineries in operation. Seven years earlier Sale & Company of London, Royal Dutch Shell and Standard Oil were purchasing Soviet oil for sale in Western markets.

Much the same pattern can be traced in the exploitation of Russian coal, though here a rather shadowy French organisation, Union Miniere, led the way under different names. As there had been considerable French investment in this field before the war, and as the Soviet Union had repudiated all debts and obligations contracted during the Czarist regime, it will be seen that care had to be taken to work under cover. Other coalfield concessions were granted to Japanese companies and also to the Anglo-Russian Grumant Company, Bryner Co. Ltd. (U.K.), Alti Formi and Acciaterie of Italy and a somewhat mysterious outfit called the Polar Star Company. Germany's Thyssen and Koppers A.G. supplied much of the equipment. The American firm, Stuart, James & Cooke, designed a five-year modernisation plan for the Soviet coal trust Comigee, while two other U.S. companies, Allen & Garcia and Roberts & Scharper, undertook to open mines and sink new shafts. Once again German firms, including Thyssen A.G., provided much of the equipment, as did Krupps, Sullivan, Allis-Chambers, Westinghouse and, needless to say, General Electric. During the period covered by Sutton, the amount of coal being mined in the Don basin increased by three thousand six hundred per cent.

In the development of the Russian iron and steel industry, Britain's huge Lena Goldfields Ltd. obtained a concession to operate blast furnaces and steel works in the Urals, where a German firm, Bergman, was busy restoring metal plants and manufacturing heavy machinery, together with guns, shells and small arms for export. Lena Goldfields also re-opened the pre-war Ridder mine complex for the production of lead-zinc. The powerful Deutsche Bank of Germany provided long-term loans. Bryner & Company (U.K.) contributed to meet Soviet foreign exchange through the export of zinc concentrates and two years after the period covered by Sutton a smelter built by Lena produced thirty-four per cent of the total Russian output of zinc.

United States technicians, hired by the hundred, re-established the Russian copper industry, with much support from Lena Goldfields, Germany's Siemens and other Western companies. Soon the entire output of silver was produced by foreign concessionaires, while Lena Goldfields Ltd. was responsible for more than one-third of Russian gold, and later for doubling total gold production in that country. Gold mining concessions were also given to other British, American and Japanese companies. Technical assistance agreements with the French and German firms by 1930 had covered most aspects of the manufacture of aluminium, and a subsidiary of the International Mica Company, Inc. (U.S.) exploited Russia's largest mica deposits.

Further detail would be tedious. It is sufficient to record that the mechanisation of Russian agriculture, the making of office-equipment (not only typewriters but even down to pens), lumber activities, locomotive and sewing-machine building, electrical plants of every kind, including telephones, the entire range of chemicals, rubber products in fact all things pertaining to modern economic life — were supplied by the capitalist world against which the Soviet Union was depicted as waging war. Firms other than those mentioned above were Ford Motors, Swedish General Electric, Ericcson (Sweden), Brown-Boverie (Switzerland), Holm (Sweden), the British Vickers-Armstrong Company, Baldwin Locomotive Works (U.S.A.), the Singer Sewing Machine complex, Dubert & Robinson (both U.S.A.), Underwood Company (U.S.A.), Stein A.G. (U.S.A. and Germany), Albert Kahn (U.S.A.), McClintock & Marshall (U.S.A.), Citroen (U.S.A.), Casale Ammonia S.A. (Italy), General Electric Company of New Jersey, Superfostat (Sweden) and innumerable others. Mention should also be made of the leading part taken by the Chase National Bank.

All the time capitalism was building up the Soviet Union the propaganda media of the West were thundering denunciations of Communist Russia. Yet the major role of the industrial giants in America and Western Europe was on so large a scale that it could not be hidden and must have been known to the national newspapers of every land. Why did they take so much trouble to conceal it from their readers? The answer, I am sure, is not that they themselves were part of the conspiracy, but fear of the tremendous Capitalist forces which by bringing pressure to bear upon their advertisers could have driven them into bankruptcy.

Newspapers apart, was there indeed a Capitalist-Communist conspiracy? Beyond doubt there was. As we have seen Schiff, the Warburgs, Otto Kahn and other members of Kuhn, Loeb & Co. and their associated concerns had been up to their eyebrows in the plot to start the Russian Revolution, for which purpose they furnished Trotsky with ample funds, placed at his disposal two hundred professional revolutionaries trained in New York, and secured for him from the British Government safe-conduct from Newfoundland to Russia. The Warburg brothers operating in Hamburg had no difficulty in persuading the German Government to allow Lenin and his colleagues, exiled in Switzerland, to be repatriated by sealed train.

Since that time the nexus between large-scale Capitalism and Communism has never been broken. The farming-out of contracts described in this chapter was not done fortuitously: only the big international corporations within the magic circle of patronage around Kuhn, Loeb (with the possible exception of Ford Motors) were allowed to participate in the exploitation of revolutionary Russia.

The process was continued in the 'thirties and stepped up enormously during the Second World War, when a huge proportion of American and British production was devoted to the needs of the Red Army, and among much else embraced the sending to Russia of processed uranium and case-loads of atomic-energy formulae. We may be quite sure, when the full truth is known, that the Soviet Union's nuclear achievements received from outside much more than the help provided by Harry Hopkins (Baruch's man at the White House) or that consequent upon the defection of Fuchs, Pontecorvo and other nuclear physicists who had been made privy to all developments in this field in the United States, Great Britain and Canada. Not all the German rocketeers of Peenemunde, however, were grabbed by the Americans: Moscow collected its fair share and subsequently had a clear field of recruitment in Eastern Germany.

I stress this point for a special reason. The Russians are a great and gifted people who have made a superb contribution to European literature and music, but in terms of modern technology--achievements in outer space notwith-standing—there is much evidence that they are laggards. During the 'thirties, when capitalist activity was if anything stepped up, British engineers who went to install machine-tools and a large range of other complex equipment in

Magnetogorsk and other areas of industrial activity, would often return a year or two later for the purpose of servicing. It was a common experience for them to find their beautiful machines ruined beyond all possibility of repair.

When the United States entered the last war it sent high-powered executives to ascertain what industrial help was needed. On the chief mission was a competent and politically disinterested journalist, L. White. White noted with amusement that when something went wrong with the sophisticated machinery imported from Britain or elsewhere — a fault occurring in a conveyor-belt, let us say—the Russians, instead of having it repaired, would station a factory worker at the spot to negotiate the conveyance by hand, thereby wasting his time day after day, month after month. It would be miraculous if a people so industrially backward were transformed by magic within a couple of decades to become a "super-power" exploring the mysteries of outer space. Beyond doubt, full use has been made of Teutonic skills reinforced by expertise from both sides of the Atlantic and largely reliant upon Western scientific instrumentation.

Should this assertion be questioned, the sceptic is asked to enquire why the capitalist world had to build up pretty well the entire Soviet economy in the inter-war period, produce prodigious quantities of armaments of all kinds to keep the Red Army supplied during the second war and obligingly make available blue-prints, enriched uranium and highly-skilled defectors to furnish Russia with its nuclear capacity after the war.

So far from Capitalist - Communist collusion having diminished during the post-war years, it has increased beyond reckoning, partly because of the Western inventive boom which has accompanied computerisation and other great advances in the electronic field, and even more because of the vast new area thrown open to outside capitalist exploitation by the Soviet conquests of what have become known as the Iron Curtain countries. It is doubtful whether a single giant international corporation based in America or Europe does not have one or more large-scale factories and selling organisations working at full blast in Russia, or Poland, or Czechoslovakia or wherever it may be. When Mr. Kruschev made his famous threat to the Western nations, "We shall bury you", I remarked to a friend: "Tomorrow the planes will be hurtling towards Moscow with representatives of every capitalist manufacturer of excavators begging for the contract!" Perhaps the idea is not as fanciful as it then seemed.

Nor was investment a one-way traffic. The use of numbered accounts in the Zurich branch of the Bank of Switzerland was an admirable device for enabling the Soviet Union to participate in the profits of Western capitalism and it may be significant that when in 1971 the question arose in Switzerland about the desirability of discontinuing the numbered accounts system it was preceded by Moscow's decision to put aside pretence and announce the formation of a Central Bank to operate throughout the Communist world, offering high rates of interest to attract capital from the West.

Thus has the wheel turned full circle and the assertion that Communism and Capitalism are as "the fell incensed points of mighty opposites" is exposed as the biggest lie in human history.

Chapter 10

# PARTITIONING THE WORLD

If the facts (even without the one or two assumptions) contained in the last chapter be accepted, it will be seen there is no need to ask on which of two sides Communists and Monopoly-Capitalists are ranged. Circles have no sides. About twenty-five years ago, when only a very few of us had caught a glimpse of this situation, Mr. Sydney Saloman, the public relations officer of the Board of Deputies of British Jews, wrote a scornful letter to the Journal of the Institute of Journalists attacking me for my belief that Capitalism and Communism were working in cahoots. I think that today not even a journalist as naive as Mr. Saloman would consider it safe to question so well established a truth.

Indeed, even at that time—assuming complete ignorance of how the Russian Revolution was financed and of the extent to which capitalist industries had built up the Soviet economy—no politically informed person should have failed to take heed of the betrayal of the West at the Yalta Conference. It was here that Roosevelt (with the Soviet agent Alger Hiss beside him as his adviser) and Stalin reached unanimous decisions about the post-war world—by the simple expedient of allowing Stalin to dictate the terms. The consequences were dire. Russia was admitted into the European heartland, establishing control of all the Eastern European countries, foremost among them Poland (for whose freedom we had supposedly gone to war) and Czechoslovakia (on whose behalf the British Left had screeched at Neville Chamberlain for not going to war). No such screech was heard when the new dispensation became known.

American acquiescence at Yalta was not a departure in policy, which had been officially launched in 1932, when Roosevelt became President of the United States and intensified after the United States entered the war. Unofficially, of course, there had been collusion ever since 1917. The publication of the Yalta records has confirmed that the partition of Europe was an act of deliberate betrayal, but what has still to be ascertained is when and where the decision was taken to divide the world. We know that at the Potsdam Conference it was agreed that Russia should declare war on Japan, by which means she was able to take control of Manchuria and launch Mao Tse-Tung and his "agricultural reformers" against the armies of Chiang Kai-shek. It could be that there was a simultaneous agreement that General Marshall should go to China to demand that Chiang join with Mao in forming a "Popular Front". As experience in Eastern Europe has shown, this was the deceptive formula used for Communist take-overs. When Chiang refused, he was left to his own devices and soon the mainland was in Mao's hands. President Nixon's visit to Peking marked the completion of another circle.

China apart, the Russo-American decrees for partitioning the rest of the world can only be surmised from the policies which were in fact pursued. They stemmed, without exception, from Lenin's well-known dictum that the European countries could best be attacked at the periphery. Holland was the first victim. Denied the right to withdraw her own ships from the Allied shipping pool, she could not send troops in time to deal with the puppet government left behind by the Japanese in the East Indies, and further hounded by Mountbatten, she had to relinquish her hold. Indonesia, the name of the successor regime, was at once supplied arms by the United States and the Soviet Union, both of which powers secured bases in that area. That this chain of events lacked design is an untenable proposition.

The second victim was France. While the French were fighting the Communists in Indo-China, their treacherous American ally slipped in by the side-door, established relations with the governments of Vietnam, Cambodia and Laos and within a short time the French were ousted, to be replaced by the Communists in the North and the Americans in the South. The next campaign against the French was to get them out of Algeria, which not only lay very much nearer France but which also had the advantage of a large French population.

"American" support for FLN, the Algerian resistance movement, incited them to open rebellion and Paris was about to hoist the White Flag when the first "Generals' Revolt" occurred and succeeded so well that the French Government fell. Thereupon the Generals asked de Gaulle to re-enter public life, confident that in his hands *Algerie Francaise* would be safe. They were reassured by his statement that never in his life-time would the FLN flag fly over Algeria. It was hoisted within the next twelve months, while Mon General was still very much alive. Then came the second "Generals' Revolt", when President de Gaulle had them—the men who brought him to power—arrested. Capitalist support for the FLN has been mentioned: how did this tie-up with Communism? Most curiously. In negotiating the hand-over of sovereignty de Gaulle secured a treaty whereby France was to continue using Mers-el-Keber, Algeria's powerful naval base. It may have been to further his quaint idea of a European Federation from the Urals to the Atlantic seaboard that Mon General agreed to abrogate the treaty several years ahead of schedule. Thousands of Soviet technicians immediately moved in!

Great Britain's abandonment of her responsibilities in the Indian sub-continent and Burma could have been predicted when the Church Government, on U.S. pressure, sent the wartime Cripps mission to Delhi. The journeys up and down the African continent of Adlai Stevenson offering aid to its many territories if they would make a bid for independence and implement the doctrine of "one man one vote" resulted in the establishment of "freedom" on the grim basis of "one man one vote—once". This has in turn led to the abolition of temperate European governments everywhere north of the Zambesi and a splitting of Africa between the take-over bidders. Abyssinia is now largely a Russian sphere of influence, Tanzania and Somaliland were placed -- fantastic though it may seem — under some kind of Chinese suzerainty, while the Belgians were ousted from the Congo to allow America under United Nations auspices to become the covert controllers of that mineral-rich country.

In *The New Unhappy Lords* I described the successful techniques employed to dispossess the Europeans of their overseas interests. Here I am more concerned with the post-war partition of the world. It is impossible to believe that what took place did so by some fortuitous concourse of circumstances. Allocation of the new spheres of influence must have been planned, there must have been collusion. How did the Chinese, who lack sea and air power and who have no industrial culture, become involved in the development of East Africa when all their efforts were needed to cope with the vital need to develop their own country? Such involvement could only have been reached by prior agreement of Washington and Moscow. One day light may be thrown upon this aspect of the conspiracy, but as things are we have only remote clues to what took place. I now relate how one such fleeting glimpse was afforded me.

Not long after the war, when I was Deputy-Editor of *Truth*, there called upon me by appointment a man who described himself as a Somali. Lacking height and the aristocratic features of the true Somali, he seemed to me to be of mixed blood or perhaps a Midgan (a tribe subjugated by the Somalis and living amongst them). Knowing Somaliland fairly well, I put to him some questions, his answers to which made clear that he also knew the country. His visit was to seek my help in tracing a wealthy Englishman who between the wars reputedly aspired to play a Lawrence of Arabia role in North Africa. Did I know his address? I did, but explained that before effecting an introduction it would be necessary for me to be told what business he had in mind.

"We want him to put up money for the creation of a resistance movement in British Somaliland."

"Resistance against whom?" I enquired. "It has been my belief that we liberated British Somaliland four or five years ago."

"Liberated from the Italians, yes", he told me. "But the time has now come for its liberation from the British, so that it can be made part of a new nation—Somalia."

"Do you seriously suggest that I should help you in your anti-British activities?" I asked.

"It cannot be anti-British because the British Government has agreed," he declared. "The Italians are to be allowed back and given a period of ten years in which to liquidate their interests and create a national feeling among the Somali tribes, including those in British Somaliland."

"When was this arrangement made?" I enquired incredulously.

"I cannot tell you that," was the reply.

"If the British Government has agreed to relinquish British interests, why should you require finance for a break-away movement?"

"The difficulty is with the Dolbahhanta (the main tribe in the then British Somaliland). As long as they can be assured of their grazing rights, they are hostile to any change and wish to remain under British protective rule. This attitude has to be changed, because your Government feels that it would be easier to relinquish control to a resistance movement than to withdraw from a friendly country."

I then took a shot in the dark. An officer who had served with me in the Somaliland campaign had stayed on as a district commissioner. Mentioning his name, I asked my visitor if he had ever met him.

"Yes," came the reply. "He is a friend of mine. I know him well."

"Then doubtless you are aware that he is a card-carrying Communist." I cut short my visitor's embarrassment by seeing him through the door!

I have no knowledge that the British Government at that early stage was a party to its own demise in the horn of Africa, but as everything else the Somali agitator said came to pass it is difficult to avoid the conclusion that the State Department, the Kremlin and Whitehall had not waited until the war's end before drawing up a geo-political map of the post-war world from which Great Britain, by her own agreement, had been virtually eliminated. My suggestion, of course, is not that a then non-existent Red China had been allocated East Africa, but that these regions could have been assigned to the Soviet Union and in due course, perhaps more for cover than anything else, made over to Peking.

Whether or not this view be correct, the one certainty is that a complete accord about the allocation of the spoils of war must have been agreed between Washington and Moscow before, during or immediately after the Potsdam Conference. Inasfar as the British Government acquiesced, it bowed to *force majeure* exerted by the New York Money Power and did so in a glow of righteousness because the liberal decay, now rampant, had assailed Attlee and his left-wing cohorts long before the war. Did it and does it not preach the Brotherhood of Man? If the concept means anything at all it must surely embrace such brotherly acts as the wholesale slaughter of millions of brethren by brethren, the sweet Mau Mau family, the putting of White brothers by Black brothers feet-first through saw-mills in Angola, the organised amok-run of Mao's Red Guards in the so-called "cultural revolution" and all such fraternal pleasantries. When British and French forces returned to Suez in 1956 to re-establish order in the Canal Zone a howl of rage went up from the international camp. The threat of financial sanctions by Wall Street, accompanied by the Kremlin's threat (palpably bluff) of intercontinental missiles, brought the cringing British Government to heel. Since that time Egypt has ceased to be Britain's sphere of influence. The Russians are now in total over-all control.

To maintain in the face of all this evidence that the changes in the world's power-structure have been adventitious and not the outcome of a conspiracy between the formidable International Money Power based in New York and its outlandish offshoot based in Moscow is to be more than a fool. It is to be culpably blind.

Chapter 11

# THE WILL TO LIVE

While the post-war map postulated in the previous chapter may require minor revision in the world of today —for instance, the partitioning of India which created Pakistan and the subsequent partitioning of Pakistan which created Bangladesh—the central features remain. The Lenin doctrine of the attack on the periphery of the European nations has had —with the until recent solitary exception of Portugal—over-whelming success. Whatever remnant of British, French or Dutch influence may be found in Asia or Africa is confined to administrative, legal or linguistic usages derived from the past: all power of control has been destroyed. There is, however, no such thing as a power-vacuum, and those who suppose that it has been filled by the local demagogues who strut upon the stage (if Cadillacs can be used for strutting) make a profound mistake. The new imperialism is based very largely on the New York technique employed to keep Central and South America in line. Let an African autocrat put a foot wrong and there is always waiting behind the scenes a "General" or a "Colonel" cognisant of the required form to unfurl the banner of revolt and introduce the same autocracy under another name, but this time with a clearer financial insight into Big Brother's will.

The pattern has been repeated so often throughout Africa north of the Zambesi that to give too many examples would be wearisome. Whereas the former imperial powers were much concerned with the establishment of sound administrations and due processes of law, their successors acknowledge no such responsibility. The immediate political aim to abolish the European empires having been achieved, they concentrate their effort on exploiting the mineral wealth of the countries they control and as long as loans and "aid" or whatever it may be are accepted, and whatever concession may be sought granted, they are happy to leave domestic issues and the panoply of government to selected "Generals" or "Colonels" or "Doctors" who have mastered the technique of terrorism to impose their will.

The peoples of Britain and the other Western nations take all the coups and countercoups in their stride. They are so conditioned by the liberal sickness that they even sympathise with these upheavals, however barbarous, and look upon them as mere teething-troubles — troubles which they are led to believe, through some unfathomable mental process, are the legacy of the "Wicked Imperialists". That European rule rescued the Africans from the sloth, the diseases, the cruelty, the miserable poverty, the superstitious horrors of mankind in its primitive beginnings, is not a line of thought which finds acceptance in the liberal mind, so that the rapid reversion to type and the hastening return under the thinnest veneer, into primeval darkness makes no impression. Indeed, the poor deluded West (except the element which thrives upon the delusion) does not see beneath the veneer, but mistakes the tragic relapse for illimitable progress on a world-wide scale. The delusion is fantastic.

One African example may serve to illustrate this truth. In another book I have described how the "youth movement" of the "enlightened" Dr. Kenneth Kaunda were sent ahead of the European-led police to deal with the villagers of a religious sect which followed the teachings of one Alice Lenshina. Those men, women and children not burned to death in their huts were most foully and obscenely killed by other means. This year (1972) Mr. Michael Wright, an English University lecturer who spent three years in the country, has written a book entitled *Zambia — I Changed My Mind*. He declares that the Kaunda Government has become "a mixture of high-flown phrases and piratical looting". Describing various violent crimes he says: "The police indeed are powerless and guns are available to criminals through their distribution to 'freedom fighter' camps and from the Congo. Violence has become commonplace again".

He gives the further information that disease and malnutrition are common now that the Government has bungled the farming situation. As far as can be ascertained, four out of ten children born in Zambia die in infancy and another two are crippled mentally or physically by lack of food. In the spring of 1970 the author wrote and I quote his words: "President Kaunda was faced with the collapse of his farming programme and with the failure of industry and the continuance of tribal dissension. Yet his main item of interest was the organisation of the Lusaka conference of non-aligned nations, as he spent a reported R12-million on it. The politics of this were simply the politics of a diversionary tactic, so typical of Black Africa. Its aim is to give the minds of the people something to think about to divert them from the real problems at hand. Perhaps, even, in Black African terms, what I would call the 'real problems' would not be seen as such." Mr. Wright's disillusionment began when he discovered that the Zambian Constitution, on which he lectured students, was totally irrelevant to either the Zambian situation or the way in which the country is run.

The author's inclination is to write the whole place off. I quote him further: "The President, riding about accompanied by Jaguar cars that were originally supposed to be used for suppression of crime, and spending thousands on a gymnasium for himself, was just the smoothest hypocrite of them all. He had launched upon a programme of folly and extravagance, and thrown open the diminishing resources of his country to the henchmen of the ruling party." It is hoped that this portrait of her hero will be brought to the notice of the British woman Member of Parliament who declared that to mention the name of the Zambian Sir Galahad and that of Mr. Ian Smith in the same breath was "infamous"!

Mr. Wright's summing-up is that the Africans have been placed in a false position by "the British impatience in doing good". He writes: "Decolonisation confronted them with a demand to function in a nation state in ways for which they were quite unsuited. The people concerned are unable to see themselves apart from their communities, and unable to run the sort of parliamentary debate and state system that we in Britain have, because each group wants to run its own affairs, and is unable to accept a decision, taken by some as applying to all."

It gives the present writer no pleasure to claim that many years before Mr. Wright made his discovery, he was the only political commentator in Britain to predict precisely what would happen, not only in Zambia but throughout the whole of Black Africa. In his classic work, *The Decline of the West*, Oswald Spengler declares that "it is impossible to impose one culture on another", and, in as far as a constitution is derived from a culture, that in essence was what the Lancaster House conferences set out to do. The imposition was not to be through force of arms but through the inordinate vanity and ambition of Black "wide-boys" who had turned into synthetic Europeans for the purpose of becoming Presidents and Prime Ministers.

As Spengler foresaw, and as Mr. Wright has discovered, it does not work. It does not work in Zambia. It does not work in any other African-governed country. It can never work and all pretence to the contrary only conceals the reality that it is not meant to work. What is intended is the creation of chaos in readiness for the One World rulers who will enslave the Africans even more ruthlessly than the Russian and Chinese peoples have been enslaved. Meanwhile the takeover bidders are thick upon the ground to corner the wealth, while agents plan how best to make the political confusion serve the ultimate world design.

When Mr. Wright places blame upon the "British impatience in doing good", he is in fact, however little aware of it he may be, indicting the liberal sickness which has made fools of a people who, not very long ago, were the most realistic and sensible in the world. Had they not carried their flag and their language over all the seas there would not be today flourishing daughter nations speaking the English tongue in every part of the globe. Among the non-Europeans, high-caste Indian widows would still be burnt alive on the funeral pyres of their dead husbands. Heads would still be hunted in Borneo. There would be no medical science to stamp out plagues and save millions of lives in innumerable territories.

The British pioneers who discovered new lands and their successors who followed to establish sound administrations bore no trace of the present liberal malaise. They were men of strength and because of that strength they won the respect and loyalty of the indigenous peoples everywhere, who flocked to them in search of help and protection. Instead of being the hated oppressors as depicted by the propagandists of what may perhaps be called Amersovietica, they were regarded as the great bulwark against oppression. The Indian Civil Service in the days of the British Raj was the finest in the world: history knows not one as devoted, as selfless, as competent or as free from corruption.

Yet today, because of the liberal disease deliberately spread by the combined agencies of International Capitalism and Communism — two sides of the same coin — the tremendous achievements of the British Empire are derided and maligned, and the British people ludicrously conditioned to feel "guilty" about the greatness of their past. Before the 1914 war the conditioning agencies, such as the B.B.C. — governed by liberal prigs and served by a disproportionate number of outright subversives — would not have been tolerated beyond a single week.

It is an insult to the spirit of man to suppose that the survival of the fittest may be equated with the survival of the slickest in conjunction with flabby sentimentalism and systematic pretence.

The most damaging of these pretences is that a politico-economic system, described by Spengler as "exclusively Western — dynamic" can operate successfully when applied by other cultures. Exporters of that system are damaged almost as much as its importers. "Life's will" said Spengler, "is to preserve itself and to prevail, or rather, to make itself strong in order that it may prevail". It is that will which the West has surrendered with the surrendering of its world responsibilities. Where there is no will to life there is a will to death and it is this which now possesses the Western mind.

Had some Eastern Culture prevailed in the world at large, we of the West would have been wise to develop our own distinctive national psyches within its context, instead of allowing them to wither while seeking to become Buddhist monks or whatever form the Culture might have prescribed. As things are, it is the Western Culture that has prevailed, and the Asians and the Africans would have been wise to accept it as "exclusively Western — dynamic" so as to develop their own racial or tribal psyches within the protection which it affords. Instead, with overwhelming conceit of the few and primitive obeisance of the many, they have become almost everywhere ridiculous parodies of their European exemplars in everything but know-how.

Not thus does Life's will prevail.

The blame does not lie with the parodies, but with the European politicians who took the line of least resistance, and did so — those at least with any modicum of percipience —knowing exactly where it must lead.

Chapter 12

# LINE UP AGAINST SOUTHERN AFRICA

Mr. Wright describes Kaunda's extravagance in lavishing money on a big international conference in Lusaka as a typical African diversionary tactic, but in fairness it must be said that such tactics are not confined to Africa. In earlier times more than one English monarch sought to distract attention from difficulties at home by embarking for a war in France or setting forth upon a crusade to fight the Saracens. Similarly in our own times, when Harold Wilson first became Prime Minister he secured a breathing space from the many grave economic problems awaiting solution in Britain by making an issue of Rhodesia — a distant land whose affairs were outside the purview of his followers, few of whom would be able to place this brave little community on the map of the world.

However, the Wilson move was not solely diversionary. It represented — although not with this intention — a further step in the carrying out of Lenin's idea of the attack on the periphery. While Moscow was willing enough to seize spheres of influence which the Western Europeans had abandoned under duress from New York, it so happened that Wilson had a premonition that he would be called upon to go cap-in-hand across the Atlantic for loans to the all-powerful financial institutions which govern the world from Wall Street. The bullying of Rhodesia would be certain to commend the bully to the Transatlantic Overlords and so facilitate the plunge of Great Britain still further into the morass of unredeemable debt.

The Money Power, as global developments have shown, is absolutist. Having decreed that the control by European nations of overseas territories everywhere must be eliminated, it is determined to allow no exceptions. What is more, it refuses to tolerate the continuance of White rule over lands which had cut adrift from the metropolitan countries whence the Europeans had come as settlers and colonists. As things stood in 1964, and as they stand today, this wrecking policy succeeded everywhere in Asia and Africa except in Southern Africa, where "reactionary" Europeans had — and retain[4] —the hardihood to insist upon

---

[4] A.K. wrote in 1973. Rhodesia fell in 1979, Angola and Mozambique in 1975, and South Africa in 1994.

civilised government in preference to barbarism and chaos. These Southern Africa countries are South Africa which has independence both *de facto* and *de jure*, Rhodesia, which has independence *de facto*, and Mozambique and Angola, which are incorporated in the Portuguese State.

All four lands are under constant attack by the New York Money Power and its satellites, which means the rest of the world. Harold Wilson was thus well aware of the form required of him when he started his seedy regime with a blustering threat to the Rhodesians, requiring them to put themselves, their descendants and their civilised way of life at the mercy of African politicians incapable of running a modern State and whose motivation, as shown everywhere else on the Continent, is to squeeze out the European, take over his property, and keep themselves in office by intimidation and downright terrorism. The Rhodesians, not unnaturally, refused.

Thereupon, determined to assert himself as the masterful destroyer of what remained of the British world system, Wilson declared economic war on Rhodesia. He attempted to establish a blockade, froze Rhodesian assets in London, where they had been deposited on trust, and when his endeavours failed to produce results this anything but bonny warrior exhorted the United Nations to intervene and impose sanctions upon one of Britain's most loyal daughter nations. In consequence British exporters not sufficiently quick off the mark to trade under cover were replaced by foreign firms, foremost among them the French, which did not give a damn about incurring Wilson's displeasure. The British aggressor lost more than did its victim.

By a strange twist of fate the Rhodesian Front, which forms the Government and which throughout has resisted Westminster's aggression, is led by Ian Smith, built up as a towering Right-Wing champion, but who is, if anything, left of Centre and has even been described by many as a liberal. That was the view of William Harper, who expressed it to me when he was still a member of the Rhodesian Cabinet. Ian Smith is a very likeable man, seemingly candid, with a fine R.A.F. record, by profession a farmer and a politician who gives the initial impression of having great strength of mind and fixity of purpose. Surveying his record over the years, however, one can but wonder whether he is altogether naive and as such suggestible, variably influenced from day to day, or else as tricky a practitioner as anybody who ever entered the political game. At one time he declared that there would never be African rule in his lifetime. A few months later he said that the Africans would not be ready to take over at the next election, but perhaps at the election after that. There is no doubt that when he initialled the H.M.S. Tiger agreement he caused Wilson to believe that he had been persuaded to give effect to it. Wilson failed to take into account that Smith would have to carry his Cabinet with him! There is still less doubt that Commonwealth Secretary Bowden was speaking the truth when he told the House of Commons that he and Ian Smith had spent half an hour in Salisbury discussing how best "to ditch the Rhodesian Front Right Wing" and that Smith in this context said that there were about thirty people who were an "embarrassment" to him.

When Labour made way for the Conservative Government, it was understood in Westminster and Whitehall that Britain's "Five Principles", the first of which was "unimpeded advance to majority rule", were unacceptable to Prime Minister Ian Smith. A year later, after the visit to Salisbury of Lord Goodman (a strange choice as British negotiator) followed by a meeting with Sir Alec Douglas-Home which led to the final "Agreement", it was apparent that the Five Principles, which were embodied therein, had become eminently acceptable both to him and to his Government.

Because their Prime Minister had stood up to the British Government and — albeit with much hesitation — gone so far as to sponsor Rhodesia's Unilateral Declaration of Independence, he became the idol of most of his Rhodesian Front supporters, who looked upon his many tergiversations as no more than wiliness. "Good old Smithy" would see them through all the perils confronting them — that was their faith and it did not desert them when the "Agreement" reached with Douglas-Home was published. That any intensive study of the document must reveal it as a blue-print for a crash educational course to secure at first parity, and soon thereafter African majority rule, did not impinge upon many of them. "Leave it to good old Smithy, he knows what he is doing". Nevertheless the more percipient members and ex-members of the Rhodesian Front had long been restive. Informed by the brilliantly edited journal *Property and Finance*, and led by the courageous Candour League of Rhodesia, the genuine Right-Wingers began some years ago to take a closer look at "good old Smithy", with results which were far from reassuring. During my last speaking-tour of the country I sensed their disquiet and asked Mr. Ian Smith whether all was happy on the Right. He gave me to understand that no trouble would be forthcoming from that direction and added that his task was now to woo the Centre. I ventured to point out that his overwhelming majority of the elections suggested that the Centre had not only been wooed but won. He agreed, but said that there was still some distance to go, which led me to ask whether what he had in mind was the wooing of the Financial Left. At this juncture his secretary promptly intervened to inform the Prime Minister that he was ten minutes late for his next appointment!

The question unanswered then has been answered now. Rhodesia's Financial Left is represented by the multi-racial Centre Party, which has come out strongly in favour of the Agreement. So has the Party's (behind-the-scenes) animating spirit, Harry Oppenheimer, the South African multi-millionaire and Rothschild associate. "If I were a Rhodesian", he declared, "I would vote in favour of the Agreement". It has been said that round about the time of the Pearce Commission the Rothschild[5] member of "Anglo-American" spent a weekend on Ian Smith's farm.

Advent of their new allies must have given the Rhodesian Front quite a shock, although not enough — at any rate as yet — to disillusion them about the ability of "good old Smithy" to see things through to a successful conclusion. Those already disillusioned could not but have experienced an intensified feeling of living on quicksands against a Wyndham Lewis background of dissolving scenery. Not only was the underlying purpose of the Rhodesian Government open to grave question, but its method of pursuing it was ham-handed beyond belief. While there is nothing — nothing whatsoever — that I would wish to say in favour of Garfield Todd or Judy Todd, to arrest and imprison without charge a former Rhodesian Prime Minister and his daughter at a most sensitive time, with the eyes of the world focused on the country was as maladroit an act of "statesmanship" as could be imagined.

No less lunatic was the belief, presumably held by the Rhodesian as well as by the British Government, that the problem could be satisfactorily resolved by the despatch of a handful of worthy Commissioners to travel vast distances, explain complicated constitutional proposals to primitive peoples completely unable to grasp their meaning, and then report back as to whether or not the Agreement was generally acceptable. African demagogues, anxious for the Cadillac-pomp of power now and not five or ten years hence, sent their couriers far and wide in advance of the Pearce Commission to impress upon the tribesmen everywhere to answer "No" and never anything but "No". At least one Commissioner, made

5 Publisher's footnote— In 1976 for Rothschild read Rockefeller.

aware of the stratagem, determined to put it to the test. "Are you in favour of the Agreement I have explained to you" he asked.

"No" roared the assembled Africans.

"Are you in favour of African majority rule?" he asked unexpectedly.

"NO" roared the Africans, remembering their brief.

Humorous though such incidents seem, they serve to underline the immense tragedy that the fate of an entire Continent has been and continues to be determined by antics which would be considered far-fetched in even the most outrageous farce. Only one thing is certain — whatever the outcome of the present negotiations, Rhodesia will remain under siege until one of two things happen — either the country will be handed back to barbarism or world-wide counter-revolution will rescue not only Rhodesians, but the whole of mankind, from the diabolism which already embraces half the earth and is encroaching with speed upon the half where freedom and rational behaviour are still able to exist. As yet, the counterattack is not even a speck on the horizon.

Mozambique and Angola, which have been Portuguese territories for upwards of three hundred years, are under international pressures no less strong and are plagued with an African fifth-column very much stronger and better equipped to conduct ruthless terrorist campaigns outside the main areas of settlement. Whereas Rhodesian troops and police, reinforced by police detachments from South Africa, are well able to cope with armed gangs sent across the Zambesi from Zambia, the Portuguese authorities in both East and West Africa have to contend not only with vast coastlines but also with the frontiers of hostile countries. Across the Rovuma River lies Tanzania, now a combined Russian, Chinese and Israeli sphere of influence, whence supplies and directives without much difficulty reach the rebel Frelimos, while to the north of Angola is Zaire, as the former Belgian Congo is now called. When United Nations authority replaced that of Belgium, guerrillas were sent across the border from the Congo to join with indigenous thugs and create one of the worst reigns of terror of recent times. One form of "amusement" was to put captured European men, women and children feet foremost through circular sawmills.

That sinister internationalist forces have been behind the subversive movements in southern Africa, as everywhere else, is not open to doubt. The attack on Rhodesia has been staged by British Governments in pawn to New York. As there is no metropolitan government to wage economic war against Mozambique and Angola (both being an integral part of Portugal) other agencies have had to be found to do the dirty work. It should be noted that the New York Money Power never directly intervenes. Students of the Congo take-over will recollect that the agencies used were the United Nations for military purposes, and for economic purposes a strange facade mostly provided by Swedish capitalism in covert liaison with the State Department in Washington. Similarly covers have had to be found for the attempt to drive the Portuguese out of Africa. Mention was made in an earlier chapter of the disgraceful part played by the World Council of Christian (sic) Churches in giving aid and comfort to terrorist movements deployed against the Portuguese authorities and, when challenged, putting forward the ludicrous excuse that the guerrilla leaders had given their "assurance" that the money provided would not be used for the purchase of arms. Since then, another provider of help for the terrorist cause has entered the arena — somewhat surprisingly, Denmark.

A small and uninfluential country, Denmark in contemporary times has been content for the most part to develop its dairy interests and wallow, totally uninhibited, in pornography. There is no obvious reason why the Danes should now aspire to work for the return of all Africa to the barbarism prevailing before the advent of the White man. The only explanation which makes sense, and which accords with the general pattern, is that the Financial Left, at war against Christian civilisation, has found yet another political pander to do its bidding.

The general "case" against the southern African states, mostly upheld by people in total ignorance of their problems, is a dislike of the colour-bar, which separates as far as possible the different communities in an attempt to avoid inter-racial friction. In the Portuguese territories, however, the colour-bar does not exist. Africans who meet the required standard are termed "evolves" and are as free as Europeans to participate in the life of the territories. Between those who qualify and those who do not there is very much less difference than there is, say, between the occupants of council-houses in Britain and members of the Athenaeum Club! That Portugal in Africa is nevertheless under as unrelenting attack as are her neighbours is conclusive proof that the objective of their enemies has nothing whatever to do with the colour-bar, but is solely concerned to destroy all European rule in Africa.

The main target, of course, is the Republic of South Africa, whose position is both immeasurably stronger and at the same time commensurately much weaker than that of her allies to the north and east. Her strength lies in the four million Whites within her frontiers, their strength of character and their know-how in exploiting the country's enormous mineral wealth and running a sophisticated modern economy. South Africa's racial policy differs from that of her neighbours. Rhodesia to some extent has become a multi-racial country in the sense that Africans sit in Parliament and by and large the Rhodesians are prepared for an extended African representation as long as it stops short of majority rule. The Portuguese in East and West Africa willingly accept "evolves" as equal citizens and insist only that the final authority reside in Lisbon.

The South African solution (if such it proves) was founded on an idea put forward as long ago as 1947 by the late Hendrik Verwoerd, the Prime Minister stabbed to death in his seat in Parliament by an assassin whose motives (and inciters) remain unknown. It provides for separate development within the home lands of the various Bantu peoples and, concerned only with local affairs, the possibility is that the scheme would have worked. As things are — and apparently without reference to happenings everywhere north of the Zambesi — these territories were promised unconditional sovereignty, which in effect means the splitting of the unitary South African Republic into eight different nations, increased to eleven now that Britain has withdrawn from Basutoland (Lesotho), Bechuanaland (Botswana) and Swaziland. In other words, White South Africa will have to contend with large enclaves and in places be infringed by independent African states in total control of their own military and police forces, their own representatives in the United Nations, their own contracting of international loans and their own foreign policies.

Her weakness, paradoxically, relates to this very strength in that the build-up of the international forces arraigned against her, already considerable, will almost certainly continue until it becomes a gigantic conspiracy assailing her at every level and in every sphere. Pressure has been continuously applied from outside since the last war with the object of trying to enforce the one-man-one-vote principle and thereby accelerate the take-over process. After Harold Wilson declared economic war on Rhodesia the coxcomb next turned his attention to South Africa, attempting to sabotage the Simonstown Agreement whereby the Royal Navy shared with the South African Navy the task of guarding the all-important Cape route to Australasia and the East. At the same time he ratted on the undertaking to supply Phantom fighters to the South African Air Force, which enabled France to put forward her Mirages in their place.

Another approach route for the attackers was the future of South-West Africa, which South African troops had captured from the Germans in the 1914 war and which had been handed over to South Africa for administration under League of Nations mandate, which the United Nations promptly claimed, without legal justification (which trailed a very long way behind) to include within its own benefice. The most recent development has been the visit there of the U.N.'s new Secretary-General, Dr. Kurt Waldheim, who after less than three days in the territory — several times the size of Britain — considered himself to be sufficient of an expert to return to New York and from there lecture South Africa with no better base than his own profound ignorance and lack of understanding. He had insisted upon calling South-West Africa "Namibia", a country which does not happen to exist[6] and which is palpably a device to create a nation out of over twenty races, mutually hostile, and with virtually no desire to be knit together in any federal structure.

When the crunch is reached, a start will almost certainly be made (if surrender has not already been complete) with an invasion of "South-West".

Internal subversion in South Africa itself, strongly supported from overseas, has been carried out by urban Blacks and a strangely large number of Whites, most of them racially identifiable. As the African population of the Republic is upwards of 14 million it will be seen that a general uprising would entail bloodshed and horror on a massive scale. That no such conflict has occurred is partly due to the contentment of the Africans as a whole and even more to the vigilance of General H. J. van den Bergh[7], perhaps the most brilliant security chief in the Western world, his expert staff and the strong support of the South African Government.

The complacency of the South African Government in surveying these prospects is no doubt based upon the extent to which the new states will be dependent on the South African economy, which will be a real factor, at any rate in the short-term. However, the fact that the Republic's well-proved security

---

[6] Namibia became the name of the country following its independence from South Africa in 1990.

[7] Publisher's footnote— Visits to Israel in 1976 appear to have altered the aim of the vigilance of both General and Prime Minister.

system will have no *de jure* status in the Bantu countries is a matter not lightly to be dismissed. It would be contrary to all experience if the African states do not become hot-beds of conspiracy and advance bases for the powers intent upon the wrecking of White rule in its last remaining stronghold.

While preparations were going ahead to shape the Bantustan policy, South African attitudes over other matters underwent a curious change. Rothschild finance began to pour into the country during the late 'fifties and early 'sixties, at the same time as major Afrikaner business interests became increasingly involved in the gigantic Rothschild-Oppenheimer complex. The South Africa Foundation, created as a semi-official public relations body, began to make its influence felt — perhaps in response to the initiative of Harry Oppenheimer's stricture as reported by the country's leading viewsletter *Behind the News*, brilliantly edited by Ivor Benson. After outlining Leftist policy Oppenheimer said "This is, after all, the only safe way to get rid of Dr. Verwoerd. All other methods will merely consolidate his position . . . The immediate task of the South Africa Foundation is to create an atmosphere in which it will be possible to arrange a coalition of the moderate elements in Government and Opposition... In effect, the advent of the South Africa Foundation reflects the return of big business to active politics. It is high time. My business colleagues have let the situation deteriorate for far too long. I think I can claim the main credit for this exciting vision of the new Africa, yet all that I have done really, is allow myself to be guided by the interests of Anglo-American. Are you still unconvinced? How can what is good for Anglo-American be bad for South Africa?"

The image of South Africa as presented by the Foundation was most unconvincingly and needlessly liberal. It carried no weight overseas. Yet there was a very strong trend towards liberalism inside the Republic's governing Nationalist Party which accompanied the involvement of the Party's backers with concerns such as Oppenheimer's Anglo-American and other interests — an involvement heralded as the bid of the Afrikaner to take his place in the financial sun. Within the space of little more than three years the attitude of every Cape Nationalist known to me did a complete about-turn. From being fiery opponents of the proposed grant of sovereign independence to the Bantustans they became its no less fierce proponents, arguing that in no other way could South Africa's overseas critics be appeased. Where today they would look for signs of that appeasement causes me to wonder!

Progress along the liberal path was bound to lead sooner or later to a split in the Nationalist Party. It came at the end of the last decade. The liberal element, which included the Government, described itself as "verligte" (outward-looking or enlightened) while the break-away movement was called "verkrampte" (conservative or, in the pejorative sense, reactionary). The verligtes forged ahead with their Bantustans and also set out to win friends and influence trade with the African states to the north. Instant success was had with Malawi (Nyasaland), whose President, Dr. Banda, paid a state visit to South Africa and was received with full honours —an unprecedented event and described as a major break-through. The occasion passed off without incident, despite the worthy Banda's shout of "Kwacha!" (Freedom!) when addressing African audiences. It may be that this was no more impertinent than Macmillan's notorious "winds of change" speech in Cape Town ten years previously.

That South Africa should seek trade with the other African countries seems ordinary common-sense, while politically the exchange of Ambassadors with Malawi has been done tactfully and without any observable ill-effects. What would happen in the long-term, with thirty or forty African embassies established in Pretoria, is quite another matter. It may be that Prime Minister Vorster murmurs to himself:

> *"I do not ask to see the distant scene,*
> *One step enough for me."*


The verkrampters, perhaps, have indeed glimpsed the distant scene and do not like what they see. If so, the long-term may provide them with some justification. In the short-term, however, their folly has been beyond belief. Forming a new party, they set out to woo the South African electorate (40 per cent of it English-speaking) by advocating the elimination of English as one of the two official languages. With Albert Hertzog as its leader, the party's ineptitude is not surprising. It is sad that the anti-liberal forces have found no worthier a champion.

The strangest feature of the colossal campaign launched against South Africa is that it has had its chief effects in the field of sport. South Africans, sons 'and daughters of the open air, are passionate lovers of all forms of sport, and the politically inspired demonstrations against their teams in Britain, Australia and New Zealand, together with titanic efforts to bar their participation in international sporting events, have made a much greater impression upon them than any thunderous denunciations from the United Nations. Yet overseas it is not from sportsmen that the violence emerges, but from hordes of shaggy, misshapen freaks who label themselves Maoists, Trotskyists, Castroists and the rest — freaks who probably do not know one end of a cricket-bat from the other and who would run a mile from any possibility of a rugby tackle. Nevertheless to doubt the effect of these pressures is to turn one's back on reality. The very fact that mobs confronting a team may have power, in the overall picture, to tip the balance and lead to a fatal compromise involving the life or death of a civilisation shows how very precarious are the times in which we live, and how essential it is to remain cool and strong though all the politicians blackguard us and all the hoodlums on earth converge upon us with faces contorted with rage and the ravages of "pot".

In the shifting sands of today the peoples of southern Africa may feel that they are particularly vulnerable — and indeed they are. But it is not barbarism which they have cause to fear. It is liberalism, seeking compromise after compromise which finally rots the spirit and drains the body politic of its will to live.

Chapter 13

# THE TWELFTH HOUR

As the hands of the clock approach twelve it becomes imperative for the Western European nations, particularly Great Britain and the British peoples beyond the seas, to take their bearings in this strange new world of the mid-twentieth century and discover precisely on what course the wind of change is driving them. Those who follow their own noses are apt to assume that wherever their noses happen to point is necessarily the royal road to the millennium — a lunatic belief at the best of times and in the present period of confusion and peril something much more than that, verging on criminal lunacy.

Captains of ocean-going vessels or pilots of aircraft who were indifferent to their position in space and time would very soon bring themselves and their charges to grief. Yet we allow nations, which carry all the riches of the past and all the untold promise of the future, to be navigated by coxcombs with never a thought in their heads other than to pose as men of destiny at the controls. It is truly the fact that amidst the infinitude of tasks required to keep our civilization in being nobody is responsible for plotting its course. Give any leader a big enough build-up and the assumption will be that wherever his nose points lie blue skies and summer seas. In consequence we can scarcely complain if on waking up we discover that we are about to be dashed to pieces onto the rocks.

We speak of conditioning processes, but habit is the deadliest conditioner of them all. As long as the human mind is confronted with familiar scenes it finds difficulty in believing that anything can be seriously amiss. It even becomes habituated to speeding-up. For instance, the erection of a huge block of flats or offices may completely change a familiar aspect of our daily lives, but because we have lived with it during the course of the few months of its building we take it for granted long before it is finished and an effort of the memory is required to visualise the original scene. I suspect that the reason why inflation does not more often cause revolution is to be found in this same power of habitude to condition the human mind.

Because the mind so swiftly adjusts itself to physical changes, its adjustment to changes less palpable — political, cultural, spiritual, whatever they may be — need occasion no surprise. Most people are too engrossed in earning a living or otherwise passing the time to pay much heed to the changing political pattern or to note the disappearance one after another of the traditional land-marks by which earlier generations were guided. Even so, to come suddenly upon a map of the modern world must be to the more intelligent a startling experience.

The world into which we were born was a world ordered by Christendom, in that the Americas had been colonised by the peoples of Western Europe and in that Asia and Africa had been tamed by Western Europeans and made answerable to systems of law based upon Christian principles. There was mutual advantage in the arrangement; in return for the administrative genius, standards of hygiene, medical benefits and reserves of power with which to cope with recrudescences of barbarism in far-off lands, the metropolitan countries gained control over raw materials, spheres of interest, trading posts and strategic bases, all ministering to their strength and thereby enabling them to discharge their duty towards the vast multitudes in all lands who looked to them for protection, guidance and succour.

That is the world into which we were born. But it is not the world that we now inhabit. There has been an almost total change, the full significance of which is understood by perhaps one person in every hundred thousand. The map of the modern world shows the nations of Western Europe, until the last two decades the law-givers and the torch-bearers to the greater part of mankind, precariously perched on the edge of a continental land-mass dominated, because of the deeply traitorous contrivances of Teheran, Yalta and Potsdam, by ruthless Russo-Mongol tyrants implacably warring against Christendom. I use the word "contrivance" because no other will do. The contrivance was not the work of Christian minds.

The precariousness of the Western position as shown on the modern map is vastly accentuated by another fact which the map reveals — almost everywhere the Western European nations have been, or are about to be, divested of control of their overseas raw materials, colonies, spheres of influence, trading posts and strategic bases. That they must, at the next step, be crushed into nonentity to make way for new and evil forces would seem to be a self-evident truth, were it not that the massed might of propaganda put out by the supplanters, conjoined with the apparently endless capacity of the human mind to accept without criticism whatever becomes an accomplished fact, manages effectively to inhibit thought.

Lenin long ago laid down the strategy whereby Western Europe was to be destroyed — the attack on the periphery. Readers of *Candour* are familiar with the details of how Wall Street and Moscow, working in double-harness, have carried out that attack at the expense of the British, French, Dutch and Belgian Empires. In as far as there are still a few scattered centres of resistance, however, it may be instructive to observe the enemy forces still in action.

Holland, denuded of the Dutch East Indies by the treachery of her allies, still holds the western part of New Guinea, but as the supplanters are very thorough, and cannot tolerate anything short of universal victory, it was to be expected that before long Indonesia would be armed and encouraged to break down this distant remnant of Dutch influence in the East. The build-up for the purpose is now said to be complete. Indonesia's "Defence Minister" declares that "decisive superiority" has been achieved, no doubt by the submarines supplied by Poland, the naval and air bases built with Soviet aid, and the huge base at Ambon built with American aid — a most beautiful *Entente Cordiale*!

It has all happened before, of course, this ganging up of the Wall Street and Muscovite forces: time and again the two have acted together against the citadels of Western European civilisation, to rob and denude them utterly of their overseas strength. Perhaps the most horrifying instance since Suez was the partitioning of the Middle East which presented Iraq, a British sphere of interest, as a free gift to the Soviet Union. I say "the most horrifying" because here the British Government was disclosed as being not even the victim of the plot, but rather an accessory. How otherwise explain the despatch of British troops to Jordan (as the Americans were sent to the Lebanon) instead of to Baghdad, where the rebellion was taking place and where our friends and protégés of the Hashemite Dynasty were being murdered? How otherwise explain why the British Ambassador, emerging like a hyena from the shadows before the corpses of the Iraqi Royal Family were cold, sought an instant accommodation with the murderers? How otherwise explain why the British Government took such elaborate care to ensure that the British governess at the Court, who had witnessed the massacre, was flown back in a way calculated to obviate all questioning by the Press?

In the same way the Macmillan-Macleod Administration took pride in being the prime accessory to the plot for the uprooting of British interests in Africa. How unnecessary it was for the blunderingly inept Mennen Williams to declare that African independence must be at the speed desired by Africans -- at the royal pleasure, in other words, of Mau Mau and the Congolese rapists! London and Brussels long ago conceded the principle. Even so, this little vignette depicting the increased arrogance of the American attitude is worth pondering over. It was taken from a *Daily Telegraph* report, which asserts that at a reception in Nairobi Mennen Williams "ignored White guests, including several Government Ministers and prominent businessmen. White Ministers and their wives were pushed aside by members of Mr. Williams' staff and told to stand elsewhere in the room, because Mr. Williams wants to talk privately with these Africans". There is precious little consolation in the knowledge that the officials and the settlers, many of them, were receiving precisely the kind of treatment they deserved, they having been very largely the agents of their own doom.

The fact remains that if there was the slightest reality in the American claim to be "containing Communism", the only elements in Africa capable of maintaining order and preventing a wholesale reversion to barbarism would not be thus insulted and rendered increasingly impotent to exercise the functions from which the Africans have derived such incalculable benefits. The whole disastrous spectacle admits of no explanation other than a vast takeover bid by the Money Power and its Communist foils, presaging a new partitioning of Africa but aimed more directly at the destruction and reduction to vassalage of the metropolitan countries of Western Europe.

Thus it is not only at the periphery that Lenin's attack against Christendom is being pressed home. For two decades — indeed, for over four decades in one way or another —Western Europe has been under continuous assault, and now most people seem habituated to the idea that their only defence consists in relying upon an ally who uses the alliance to dominate and subdue them. They accept without question that the supreme commands shall all be in American hands. They gave their consent to the merging of Fighter Command with Nato forces and did not complain when Bomber Command, at the instance of the Bow group of Conservatives who enjoyed Harold Macmillan's special favour and protection, was also flung into the melting-pot of the new Fred Karno's Army.

In all that pertains to sovereignty we are being wiped, like a dirty mark, out of history, but as long as there is no diminution in the supply of washing-machines, refrigerators and television sets, it is confidently expected of the British people that they shall take no cognisance of the fact. Nor is the expectation likely to be ill-founded. Never since the world began has a nation as sturdy as were the British but half a century ago become as mentally confused — indeed, as intellectually depraved — as are the British peoples in every land at the present time. If Conservative thinking on national survival is non-existent except in terms of surrender and treason, Socialist thinking of whatever school is so closely allied to gibberish that it lacks the coherence that would give it even treasonable shape. Madmen cannot betray.

The Brigadier from England who constituted the "Opposition" at one of my South African meetings — a man as gallant as he was dense, quite a familiar combination in professional soldiers — announced in a voice full of the strangest, most inexplicable satisfaction : "We British have become too civilised to rule over other people." As soon as I had recovered my breath I challenged his use of the word "civilised" and asked him whether he did not perhaps mean "decadent".

"I am not decadent", he almost shouted at me, as though by exculpating himself he felt that he was furnishing a clean bill of health for the entire British nation. Some days later my eye happened to alight on this passage from a London report in the *Cape Argus*: "Soccer grounds where hooligans throw bottles and stones at referees, punch players, chase linesmen and fight among themselves may have to be closed. The alternative is for clubs to build strong wire fences in front of the terraces. Sir Stanley Rous, the F.A. secretary, admits that the increasing number of crowd incidents is causing concern and says: 'They happen because people are getting to dislike authority more and more. I never want to see wire fences in this country. Their introduction would be a terrible indictment of our crowds'." Were these the people too civilised to rule others?

Reflecting on these frenetical mobs, and on the even windier specimens who shuffle behind skiffle-bands to Aldermaston or line up behind Fenner Brockway to demonstrate solidarity with the enemies of their country, wherever they may be; reflecting on the anti-British and anti-White bias of pretty nearly the entire British Press, and reflecting on the outright betrayal of British and White interests by successive British Governments, I wondered whether it was not my duty to seek out the Brigadier and say to him :

"Look here, old boy, you and others like you should stop being bloody fools and pretending that nothing is wrong with the British people. If you would bring to your thinking one-tenth of the robust quality you have shown on the battlefield it must become obvious to you that something is quite hellishly wrong with them. There is scarcely a single manifestation of their present-day spirit which does not stink of decay. It is the negation of patriotism to insist that to the pure of nostril the smell is really one of attar of roses. Brave deeds on the battle-field can only be derided by subsequent moral cowardice in refusing to face disquieting facts." But alas! There are so many like the Brigadier.

Midst all the confusion in which the British and the other Europeans are languishing there is evidence of a mind at work which is anything but confused. The attack on the Western nations at home and overseas has been carried out with an almost mathematical precision: one can almost see the lifting of the sights — after the Congo, Angola; after Tanganyika, Mozambique, and so on. Yet even when one has the opportunity of fully deploying one's argument it often happens that there are critics who admit all the facts and yet deny the evidence of design. What has happened, in their view, is the result of a fortuitous concourse of circumstances. The malignancy lies in our stars, not in our enemies, whose very existence may be disputed.

For the benefit of such critics — it will not take me far from the main theme — I propose to quote from a profoundly interesting *Daily Telegraph* review setting forth what had to happen before Zionist ambitions in Palestine could be fulfilled:

"For as one reads Mr. Stein's skilful narrative — and how much some professional historians could learn from this handling of a complicated story by a distinguished lawyer --- one becomes aware of the quite extraordinary concatenation of events that was necessary if the British Government was publicly to commit itself to 'view with favour the establishment in Palestine of a national home for the Jewish people'.

"It was necessary that Turkey should enter the war and remain in it long enough for the collapse of her empire in Asia to be irrevocable; it was necessary that the British should still see their future with imperial eyes and regard as intolerable the establishment of French domination within striking distance of the lifeline of Suez.

"It was necessary, further, that Russia, having accepted the Sykes-Picot agreement should not be in a position to attempt to revise it in her own favour or in the interests of Orthodoxy; it was necessary that all this should come about at a time when nascent Arab nationalism had made so little progress in the area in question, and the Arabs of the Levant should have taken so little part in freeing themselves from the dominion of the Turk, that it was possible for the major Allied Powers to feel satisfied that the Arabs, as Smuts put it, 'largely as a result of British action came better out of the Great War than any other people'.

"But above all it was necessary that the dreams of the persecuted Jews of Eastern Europe should for this brief period coincide with the dictates of British imperial strategy as seen by such men as Lloyd George, Milner and Balfour himself."

The moral of this particular story is that all the events which were required to happen did happen. Those who argue that they happened through a series of accidents are surely rather innocent people.

Much the same complex of interests which inspired the earlier conspiracy is at the centre of the present conspiracy to bring about the downfall of Christendom. That is what makes it so formidable. The brains employed in remoulding the world have no peers in the science of subversion, the resources behind them are limitless and nothing, absolutely nothing, is left to chance.

Readers may remember that some years ago Australia's Minister of Defence Townley, perhaps mistakenly briefed, boasted to me of the rapid progress being made in preparing Eastern New Guinea for independence. When I questioned the wisdom of the step, he said: "Oh yes, I agree that we White races are cutting our own throats." When I asked why we did not stop cutting our own throats, the Minister replied glumly: "World opinion." That was intended to convey a total explanation of the lunacy. I still have not made up my mind whether the Australian Minister of Defence believes that "world opinion" — the very last thing that the planners would leave to chance — is something that groweth where it listeth, or whether he knows as well as I do that it is a calculated effect of enemy propaganda. Yes, *enemy* propaganda. Mr. Townley must at least have an inkling of who the opponents of the White Australia policy are, and he cannot be so naive as to regard them as Australia's friends.

As the traditional world is progressively undermined, the new world is being prepared for our habitation and it is very far from being a brave new world. The established truths and ancient codes handed down to us by our fathers have manifestly to give way to whatever shibboleths may animate the bi-sexual pantaloons who shuffled backwards and forwards to Aldermaston. National pride can command no part in the future, for Bernard Baruch has pronounced it to be "silly". That means goodbye not only to national pride but to the very concept of nationhood. Goodbye, too, to the racial differentiation which has given such colour and diversity and richness to mankind, because that is in even worse odour than are the historic nations of Western Europe. The first chairman of the World Health Organisation ridiculed the possession of a white skin and besought every Canadian couple to adopt a coloured child.

These are no airy-fairy abstractions. Look at the policies being pushed in every land and you will see that the devils are ceaselessly engaged in carrying out, in one form or another, their own vile doctrines. Nor is the end-result an abstraction—the One World millennium of power monopoly devised by the master-usurers of New York for their exclusive glory, although doubtless with perquisites enough for the commissars and secret police who will be called upon to run the universal prison-state. How near this evil dream is to fulfilment may be judged by the extent to which our own Western societies have been rotted by subversion and treason.

Chapter 14

# TOMORROW — A PLAN FOR BRITISH SURVIVAL

The duty to sound the alarm is as imperative today as it has been at any time in the past. But the position has now deteriorated beyond the point where a general appreciation of the facts would alone be enough to avert the doom of the British nations and the ignominious surrender of the White race. Hitherto, when taxed with not offering a more constructive approach to the problems confronting the modern world, our reply has always been that when a ship is being driven on the rocks there could not possibly be a more constructive act than to draw attention to its course and demand that the engines be thrown into reverse. That in the past has always seemed to me a complete answer to our critics, but it is no longer a complete answer, for the simple reason that awareness at the present time is likely to lead not to remedial action but to paralysis. We must, for some, continue to sound the alarm about the ship being driven on the rocks, but for others, those who have been awakened to their peril, we must use all our persuasive powers to establish that the entire ocean is not rock-strewn, and that there is a practical alternative to shipwreck.

What is required is not the changing of our principles and fundamental premises — Heaven knows that these have been fully justified by the cataclysm of events — but instead a re-statement of our case in terms of policy, to demonstrate that the survival of the British world is not only desirable but possible.

First of all we must categorically reject as institutions of the enemy all internationalist agencies which limit the sovereignty of the British nations. The enactment of Dumbarton Oaks and Bretton Woods have to be recognised for what they are — attempts to suborn the peoples of the earth and make them amenable to the will of the International Money Power, ultimately as units regulated by a World Government. In the same category must be placed the various treaty organisations which sap national independence by a system miscalled interdependence, which is demonstrably another word for dependence — the surrender over a wide area of the national will. There is no reason why treaties should not survive the treaty organisations. Alliances, despite false declarations to the contrary, need not be an invasion of national sovereignty. Where they do invade national sovereignty, as in Nato, they are properly to be regarded not as defensive arrangements but as channels of control through which the Money Power regiments its subjects and makes the free exercise of their own wills impossible.

## DESTRUCTIVE ALLY

There are some readers who have still to be convinced that the dominant Money Power is to be recognised as a supranational body operating from New York, holding absolute sway over Washington and working closely with Moscow to increase or relax world tensions as this or that policy move or financial racket may require. We have produced abundant evidence in support of our contention that such a cabal exists and that its decrees have almost the force of law in the regulation of human affairs, but for present purposes, although convinced that the Americans are as much the victims of the cabal as we are, I make no protest if sceptics read for "Money Power" the words "United States". Whether or not the United States be a free agent, nobody in his senses can deny the part it has played in destroying the Western European empires, and this it has done not in the role of declared enemy but as a declared friend —our chief ally and (save the mark!) protector.

## BIG BROTHER

Therefore, leaving damn fools to believe that the United Nations, its special agencies, and the treaty organisations are run on "democratic" lines, I can at least assume that all intelligent readers will agree that Big Brother, whether depicted as Roosevelt, Eisenhower and the ridiculous President Kennedy, Ford or Carter, or as the Rockefellers, the Warburgs, Lehman, Frankfurter and other members of the immensely powerful Jewish cabal, has despoiled the Western European countries of their heritage and reduced them to vassalage — and always, as it happens, with Muscovite approval. The pattern of relationships established by the United Nations, Nato, Seato, the E.E.C. and the rest, has placed Big Brother, whether Gentile or Jew, in the position of being, if not altogether immune from criticism, at least in a position to ride rough-shod over opposition, so that we have been betrayed and imprisoned by the very devices advertised to us as a shield to protect us from adversity — in both senses, a red shield! There can be no national independence, no survival of free peoples, until these devices are utterly renounced.

Secondly, and to some readers this may come as a shock, we must categorically reject, as another institution of the enemy, the internationalist agency once known as the British Commonwealth, and now, to cushion its impact on the delicate sensibilities of Nehru and Nkrumah, described as "the Commonwealth". Even before the Prime Ministers' disastrous conferences at Lancaster House, the clamour of the Afro-Asian members made this nebulous conglomeration of peoples, united by no common allegiance, an active agent in the dissolution of the British world system. Their attack on South Africa, forcing that country into the wilderness, was in direct furtherance of the integrationist policy of the Money Power, while the final communique issued by the Prime Ministers made continued support for the Commonwealth by any informed patriot impossible. This, it will be remembered, declared that the general aim should be "nothing less than the complete abolition of the means of waging any kind of war", stressed that "disarmament should be phased to ensure that no country gained any significant advantage" and demanded both "an effective means of inspection and an international police force". Here is an outright statement of the supreme objective of the international financial cabal, outlining the main structural features of the universal prison-state that is being planned for the habitation of mankind. There is no alternative in honour to a root-and-branch repudiation of a Commonwealth that turns propagandist for so vile a cause.

Were the internationalist agencies to be smashed — or, at any rate, were Great Britain to withdraw from them — and were the Commonwealth, not before due season, to be given decent burial, what would remain? Those easily given to panic are sure to ask the question in great perturbation and alarm. The answer is simple. Common interests would remain. In place of the treaty organisations there would be a straight-forward system of alliances which neither sapped national spirit nor denied to nations their own sovereign power of decision. Great Britain, France, Holland and Belgium are all members of the Western Alliance, but no idiot could be so benighted as to suppose that their treaty organisations have helped them to give each other covering-fire in safeguarding their overseas territories: the result has been the direct opposite. Indeed, it is clear that the function of a treaty organisation is to enable the senior partner to dominate junior partners and deprive them of their capacity to protect their own interests. That is why we insist that no resurgence of the West is possible until the tyranny of supranational agencies has been overthrown.

What would take the place of a liquidated Commonwealth? Here again common interests suggest the answer. The countries once known as the British Dominions — the White Dominions — not only share a heritage which finds expression in innumerable departments of life but they require the cohesion of their world system for the proper exercise of their own national sovereignty. Strategically and economically they are so placed that, once the despotic power of Wall Street finance was broken, they could, in free association, command the future.

Leaving on one side for the time being (but only for the time being) the republican issue, good sense would demand an honoured place in this proposed nucleus for both South Africa and Southern Ireland. The adherence to the system of the present Afro-Asian members of the Commonwealth would be on terms laid down by the White nations of the British world, because these nations have been — and remain — the bulwark of civilisation in the ends of the earth and the idea of their being chivvied and harassed by the parvenu States created by High Finance in Asia and Africa is contrary to nature and repugnant to what the White race owes to its own proper dignity and pride.

Unlike all other proposed groupings, the grouping which I suggest is realistic in the sense that it already in some sort exists and public sentiment would be predisposed to welcome its sharper definition and its more vigorous functioning. What would be required above all also would be a sense of identity, a sense of common danger, a sense of common purpose. As this could only be achieved in the teeth of the mighty organs of publicity operated by the International Money Power I am certainly not disposed to argue that the task is easy. But there is no evidence that the British people, once their wits are alerted, can be intimidated by difficulties, however great. There is much evidence to the contrary.

Our first concern, therefore, must be to try to secure a clarification of the issues in the minds of all British peoples, above all those who are the inhabitants of the Motherland. Our work in the United Kingdom requires an intensification of effort, but no re-statement. The issues are clear enough —treason in high places, subservience to the New York cabal, political and military integration under American auspices, the future of Kenya and the Rhodesias, the flooding of our beautiful country by hordes of coloured immigrants. But we have to do more than cope with problems which are distinctively our own. If my thesis of a resurgent world system based on the former White Dominions is valid (and if it be not valid all work within each set of national frontiers must surely prove vain) then we have also to communicate this vision of the future to our colleagues in each of the countries concerned, persuading them that only within the context of such a system can they hope to exercise their own sovereign national wills. So devastating has been the advance of internationalism and the upsurge of fifth columnism to make common cause with it, that the task of our overseas colleagues will be as tough as our own, and in Canada, because of the extent of U.S. infiltration, perhaps even tougher.

The last war, during which so many malignant growths were fostered, gave a great impetus to the secessionist movement in Canada. Special care seems to have been taken to indoctrinate the Canadian services. A university lecturer who attained a fairly high rank in the F.C.A.F. told me that he and his brother-officers had fully made up their minds that Canada must be swung out of the British orbit. When I asked what virtue there was in leaving the British orbit only to become more deeply enmeshed in the New York network he replied: "We'll take care of that side of it". It was, of course, an empty boast. Mackenzie King, Lester Pearson and now Trudeau were engaged up to their eyes in the furthering of Wall Street policies, which included a benign attitude towards the Soviet Union and the outright championship of the bogus Zionist claim to Palestine. This was the period when Canadian seamen were put into uniforms which would distinguish them from ratings of the Royal Navy and so protect them, as the Canadian people were told, from the odium of being mistaken for Britons. What odium would that be, if not the kind manufactured by Jewry for use as long as the British tried to hold some kind of a ring for the Arabs? When dispositions came to be made for the defence of North America the Jewish cabal shaping internationalist policies in New York saw to it that Great Britain, which had fostered the development of both North American nations, should be left ignominiously out on a limb. That Pearson earned the gratitude of his masters is proved by the Israeli award to him of its Medal for Valour! In the same way the showering of Jewish honours and encomiums on Diefenbaker makes clear that Jewish honours took the change of Government in its stride. Diefenbaker's declared aim of destroying the pride of Canadians in their British ancestry and traditions reveals how brazen has become the attack on the British world.

Nevertheless, although Canada would seem to be the most overtly Jew-controlled of all the Queen's domains, there is no doubt that Canadians are alive to the threat to their nationhood represented by the infiltration of American capital and influence, and many of them are now prepared to reconsider their position in the light of experience. Diefenbaker ratted on his election promise to divert to Britain a substantial part of Canada's trade with the United States, but that he should have made it in the first place is clear evidence that such a move would be popular with Canadian voters. The truth is that there miraculously survives in Canada an abundance of good-will towards Great Britain, and it is not confined to men and women of British ancestry. We know many splendid Canadians of non-British origin who proudly accept the British heritage. Exacting though the task must prove, if Canadian loyalists show sufficient resolution they can still rescue their great country from subversive influences and regain and extend their national freedom within the context of a modern British world system.

Australia being further from New York than is Canada, the seditionists there have had a more difficult job in weaning Australians from their traditional loyalties. Even so, the attack is being successfully pressed home on many fronts and in accordance with what have become orthodox principles of subversion. The Australian Press, almost in its entirety, has gone over to the enemy. The universities might be replicas of London or Manchester or Leeds or Capetown or McGill. And when the time came for the cutting of military ties between Australia and Great Britain, the right man was in the right place — Lord Casey — to do a deal with Dulles when he was Truman's ambassador-at-large and set up the Anzus treaty, Britain's exclusion from which being specifically decreed. So short is the public memory that people today suppose that the Anzus treaty is a measure to contain Communism, whereas its pretext was the guaranteeing of American protection to Australasia on the occasion of the signing of the peace treaty with Japan! Any pretext is good enough as long as it serves to weaken the British world.

The subversive forces are now busily engaged, as was to be expected, in undermining the White Australia policy. Newspaper editors, university professors, teachers, civil servants, students, the inevitable clergymen are hell-bent on the destruction of Australia by throwing the country open to Asian immigration. In time the pressures exerted on Canberra will equal in ferocity the pressures exerted on Pretoria, and are unlikely to encounter the same stern opposition. If the vision of a re-formed and reinvigorated British world system here set forth is to be realised, the British peoples everywhere, at whatever cost, will have to take an unfaltering stand by Australia's side. As I see the future of the world, only peoples prepared to defend their values at whatever cost will survive as sovereign entities. In the meantime there are Australians, some of them very well informed, who offer battle to the International Money Power.

They would do so much more effectively if they could divest themselves of some of the more fanatical money-reform pedants who, like most of their kind everywhere, infinitely prefer heresy-hunting to fighting the enemy.

New Zealand is in much the same plight. Even Government departments there take the responsibility of bidding New Zealanders embrace an Asian destiny, while ecclesiastical fifth columnists tell them the flaming lie that they have more in common with their Asian neighbours than with their British kith and kin. Auckland on a Sunday night reveals how far "integration" has gone between New Zealanders, Cook Islanders, Solomon Islanders, Fiji Islanders and the whole Pacific shooting-match at the teddy-boy level. What is now being fostered is the guiding of the same growth into the higher social strata. As in Australia, there is a certain local opposition to the Money Power, but some of it is more idiosyncratic and less stable.

Curiously, South Africa, although riddled by conspiracy and subjected to continued bombardment by the world's Press, is in better shape, and far more self-assured, than any other nation adhering to what remains of the British system. This is not because of any general awareness of the menace of the Money Power but because one aspect of internationalist policy — that of racial integration — happens to conflict with the deepest instincts of the people. South African self-assurance, being based on tacit local agreement between the Whites, could well destroy itself through unjustified complacency. If White South Africa is to survive, it can only be by extending local agreement to sources of White power elsewhere. That is why the retention of the British world system and the resurgence of the British spirit should be regarded as of paramount importance by the custodians of civilization in the Union. The internationalist enemy cannot indefinitely be contained at the line of the Limpopo River unless his general strategy and design are more generally understood.

South African readers may spare themselves the labour of stating that the British Government is bespoke. We are not blind to realities. The fact remains that in the critical years ahead help for White South Africa is far more likely to come from the British nations than from any other quarter. South Africans would therefore be better employed in cultivating their friends than in trying (as South Africa House in London despicably tries) to appease their enemies. They should remember that a position has been reached wherein the African bridgehead established in Ghana for the attack on White civilization has been enlarged to embrace the whole of West Africa, and that a second bridgehead for subversive operations is now available in Tanganyika, where Nyerere depicts the creation of an East and Central African federation which, in his own words, "would make the South African position impossible". Indeed, even without any such federal structure the South Africans cannot hope to withstand the long continuance of Black pressures responsive to internationalist control. What is happening is war — war not only against White South Africa but against the White races. It is a war the White races cannot win unless they are prepared to fight back. One of the first signs of vitality in a resurgent British world would be an immediate alignment with the Union and an ultimatum to the rabble of "emergent States" in Africa to stop their aggression — with paratroops and mobile divisions at the ready to enforce the decree. To remain under attack without the will to counter-attack is to invite defeat, and what sort of a world would it be if the White nations were indeed defeated?

There will be those who sense danger in my proposal for the defence of Western civilisation. Of course there is danger. Danger is inherent in life. But the best safeguards against it are boldness and determination, qualities which the Western European nations have placed in the discard during the last decade and a half. What is the alternative? A rapid acceleration of policies of surrender which will make the terms of life impossible for White men and women throughout Africa and at next remove throughout Australasia, followed by the swift collapse of Christendom. If the course which I propose can be adopted before Kenya and the Rhodesias are completely returned to barbarism, so much the better. If not, then I unhesitatingly affirm the necessity for the eventual reconquest of those territories which, like the Union of South Africa, are the creations of the European genius and therefore the moral possession of their creators.

Once we returned to the robust attitudes which made our peoples great we should not lack for allies. The Western European nations would surely take heart from our resurgence and join with us in safeguarding civilisation throughout the world. Indeed, the American peoples themselves might be encouraged to make their second Declaration of Independence, this time of the Wall Street usurers who subvert and pervert the traditional European values and who are as great a menace to freedom in the United States as they are everywhere else.

I do not belittle the size of the job to be done, but I insist that the re-animation of a world system which has proved its worth, and which still in part exists, is necessarily very much easier to achieve than any of the innumerable schemes for securing the federation of nations which do not and never have accepted a common allegiance or shared the same institutions. Mention of a common allegiance brings us back to the republican issue. We Candour Leaguers are necessarily Monarchists, and nonetheless so because the classic concept of the Monarchy as the protector of the people has ceased for the time being to be a factor in our governance. On a short-term view the issue between Monarchy and Republic is irrelevant to the South African task of holding the pass for civilization. On a long-term view it could be of cardinal importance. If I am right in my assumption that the former White Dominions, in association with a resurgent Britain, offer the only possible nucleus for White unity throughout most of the world, it follows that there must be a supreme unifying factor, and that factor, I suggest, should be the British Crown. But until we again become a proud, strong, dynamic people we are in no position to ask Afrikaners to resume allegiance to their former Sovereign or even to listen to our argument for the necessity of a shared loyalty. Had the British nations taken the lead in championing White leadership in Africa, republicanism in the Union would have remained a minority movement. We have nothing by way of accomplishment in this field to commend us as a nation and as a community of nations. Undefeated in war, we have now bitten the dust in peace, and defeat (my cousin Gilbert notwithstanding) knows no magic and attracts no friends.

The day ends for us in disgrace — a disgrace which we of the Candour-League movement have striven to avert. There remains tomorrow. Let us lose no instant after the striking of the midnight hour before we return to the battle and seek a decision on the issues which we have here endeavoured to clarify. Victory is for the brave of heart and the tough in spirit. In these respects we have not the pretext that our fathers left us ill-endowed.

# About *The A.K. Chesterton Trust*

*The A.K. Chesterton Trust* was formed by Colin Todd and the late Miss. Rosine de Bounevialle in January 1996 to succeed and continue the work of the now defunct Candour Publishing Co.

The objects of the Trust are stated as follows:

**"To promote and expound the principles of A.K. Chesterton which are defined as being to demonstrate the power of, and to combat the power of International Finance, and to promote the National Sovereignty of the British World."**

Our aims include:

- *Maintaining and expanding the range of material relevant to A.K. Chesterton and his associates throughout his life.*

- *To preserve and keep in print important works on British Nationalism in order to educate the current generation of our people.*

- *The maintenance and recovery of the sovereign independence of the British Peoples throughout the world.*

- *The strengthening of the spiritual and material bonds between the British Peoples throughout the world.*

- *The resurgence at home and abroad of the British spirit.*

We will raise funds by way of merchandising and donations.

We ask that our friends make provision for *The A.K. Chesterton Trust* in their wills.

The A.K. Chesterton Trust has a **duty** to keep *Candour* in the ring and punching.

# <u>*The A.K. Chesterton Trust* Reprint Series</u>

1. Creed of a Fascist Revolutionary & Why I Left Mosley - A.K. Chesterton.

2. The Menace of World Government & Britain's Graveyard - A.K. Chesterton.

3. What You Should Know About The United Nations - The League of Empire Loyalists.

4. The Menace of the Money-Power - A.K. Chesterton.

5. The Case for Economic Nationalism - John Tyndall.

6. Sound the Alarm! - A.K. Chesterton.

7. Six Principles of British Nationalism - John Tyndall.

8. B.B.C. - A National Menace - A.K. Chesterton

9. Stand by The Empire - A.K. Chesterton (coming soon)


## <u>Other Titles from *The A.K. Chesterton Trust*</u>

Leopard Valley - A.K. Chesterton

Juma The Great - A.K. Chesterton

The New Unhappy Lords - A.K. Chesterton

Facing The Abyss - A.K. Chesterton

The History of the League of Empire Loyalists - McNeile & Black (coming soon)


**All the above titles are available from The A.K. Chesterton Trust, BM
Candour, London, WC1N 3XX, UK**